Britain
and Czechoslovakia

BRITAIN AND CZECHOSLOVAKIA

A Study
in
Contacts

by
J. V.
Polišenský

(Second
revised edition)

Edited by Boleslav Seidl
Cover and lay-out
by Miloslav Fulín

Art Editor: Věra Šalamounová

Cover pictures are from
John Speed's Map of Bohemia (1626)

Printed in Czechoslovakia
by MÍR, n. p., závod 1, Praha

Price: 9,— Kčs

Contents

St. George has been extremely popular in Bohemia
from time immemorial.

Introductory

I have had some difficulty in persuading myself to write this little book, although I have long intended to do so. Some indication of this is that nearly twenty years have passed since the first short version was published. Of course, there is the advantage that I now see more clearly the difficulties involved in such an undertaking.

The subject is one that can be treated much more comfortably in a book than in a short study. It is a fascinating story. Contacts between two distant countries and their peoples can exist, without any doubt, in several and often complicated ways. I have had to concentrate on contacts between the more representative members of the two countries involved, including a mixed company of medieval princes and princesses, bishops and revolutionaries, industrial pioneers, diplomats, scholars and politicians. Moreover, the picture of relations between the two countries would be incomplete without an outline of the indirect contacts, in other words, without the picture of each country in the other's literature.

I hope readers will agree that the historian should primarily be interested today in points of contact and inter-relationships, which does not necessarily call for a synthetic reconstruction of the whole of the past, especially in a booklet like this. Yet even so it may be possible to do away with a lot of misunderstandings and obsolete legends. We do not share the belief of an English chronicler, probably John Harrison, who wrote in 1620 of old Bohemia: "This country has had more correspondencies with England than any of the countries in the world, so far remote...", nor do we agree with the English politician who, as recently as September 1938, proclaimed that Czechoslovakia was just a far-away country about which the British people knew nothing.

The twentieth century has rightly been called a century of revolution. A revolution is also taking place in our conception of history. The technological and scientific revolution is forcing us all to rely more and more on the power of reason. The extension of reason means, moreover, the emergence into history of groups and classes, of peoples and even continents that had hitherto lain outside it. Historical science is less concerned today than in 1938 with *élites*, with privileged and underprivileged (and hence unknown) nations. And so I believe that a sober review of British-Czechoslovak relations in the political and cultural sphere has its place in historical study, which is slowly and painstakingly becoming aware of its widening horizons.

Medieval England
and Medieval Bohemia

1

Until recently European history has been predominantly the familiar story of the rise of Western national monarchies, the story of constitutional struggles, conflicts between Empire and Papacy, with Central Europe mainly represented by Germany. Today, all these problems, though real enough, no longer loom so large. The emphasis is shifting to the growth of the Feudal Order in Europe and its rise to the point where it could compete with the hegemony of the East. Thus we should in future seek to know much more of the borderlands of Eastern Europe, which felt the brunt of the Mongol incursions in the thirteenth century. We are less preoccupied with the quarrels of Empire and Papacy, and more concerned with other movements of a more universal character.

The thirteenth century can be regarded as the end of a preparatory period in the history of British-Czechoslovak relations. Their beginnings can be traced back to the days of King Alfred the Great, who in his Anglo-Saxon version of the Latin Chronicle of Orosius gives a sketch of the geography of eighth- or ninth-century Europe. Alfred was the first to write of the Slavonic tribes, then living as far west as the Elbe. He mentioned the land of the "Wineda", the Wends or Elbe-Slavs, and noted that to the south of them lay "Sysyle" (Silesia) and to the south-east "Maroara" (Moravia), reaching as far south as the Danube and the land of the Carinthians and the Vistula. "Maroara", or the Great Moravian Empire, as it is called in other contemporary sources, was the oldest West Slavonic state, and included not only the Slavs of present-day Moravia, Bohemia and Slovakia, but also the Lusatian Serbs, Poles and the Slavs in Pannonia, corresponding to the western half of present-day Hungary. Within this Empire arose the most ancient of all Slavonic cultures with Old Church Slavonic as the common written language of all the Slavs. But what were the origins of this remarkable civilization, whose centres have engaged the attention of archaeologists during the last twenty years?

Many centuries before the reign of the learned Anglo-Saxon king, Britain and Bohemia-Moravia were among the first centres of European prehistoric culture. Even their names are of the same origin. For the Boii of Bohemia and the Britons of Britain were members of the vast family of Celtic tribes which held sway over territories extending from the Black Sea to the Atlantic in the old days before Christ was born. Both countries were overrun by Teutons; first Bohemia, then Britain, which became Anglo-Celtic, and has remained such up to the present day. The third wave of conquerors was different in the two countries. The Slav invaders of Bohemia decided the ethnic structure of vast tracts of Central Europe and had nothing in common with the Romanized inhabitants of Normandy.

Even before 1066, relations between the West and the centre of the continent were by no means exceptional. Some of the oldest churches in Moravia, built from the end of the eighth century onwards, are sometimes linked with the activities of an Anglo-Irish mission coming from southern Germany. The riddle has not yet been solved: but it is probable that the origins of this culture were neither Anglo-Irish nor Byzantine, and that its roots have to be sought in the provincial areas of the late Roman Empire, especially in the area of the Balkans. Incidentally, the conflict between the Eastern (Greek) and Western (Latin) missions, each representing a different type of Christianity and connected with different structures of society, was decided in favour of the Latin type in the seventh century in Anglo-Saxon Britain, and in the tenth century in Bohemia.

There is nowhere to be found on the European continent such a powerful Anglo-Saxon influence on the local coinage as in the Bohemia of the late 10th and the early 11th century. The *denarii* of Duke Boleslav II seem a mere imitation of Ethelredian Anglo-Saxon coins, Duke Jaromír's *denarii* bear the name and title of King Ethelred II and that of Ethelred's mintmaster Aelfzige of Winchester. In Bohemia, Mělník, now known mainly for its excellent wine, was the place where coins of the same type were struck by Boleslav's wife, Princess Emma, who was the first princess in the sphere of the Holy Roman Empire to strike coins in her own mint, probably a part of her dowry. Her *denarii* are of Ethelredian type with the bust and legend *Emma Regina* on the obverse. It is impossible to accept the assertion that the Anglo-Saxon elements on the Bohemian *denarii* were the result of the commercial relations with England of the young Czech State, then the Dukedom of Bohemia, the successor to the Great Moravian Empire, destroyed one generation earlier.

On the other hand we know that King Athelstan's daughter Eadgith became the wife of Otto, later German King and Emperor. Eadgith was accompanied on her journey by her younger sister, mentioned by the Anglo-Saxon chronicler Ethelwerd and by the author of *Gesta Regum*, William of Malmesbury, who stated that the younger sister Elfgifa (Aelfgyfu) had been married to some ruler living not far from the Alps, and the learned German nun Hrotswitha gives her name as Adiva. The chief evidence of Elfgifa's marriage to the young ruler of Bohemia is her likeness on the coins and the name Adiva — corresponding to the continental form of her name known from Hrotswitha's verses. We know, moreover, that King Ethelred II's wife was called Emma in Normandy and in

England. The Anglo-Saxon Chronicle states about the year 1017 that this wife of Ethelred II was "Aelfgive in English, Ymma in French". Apparently the Anglo-Saxon Princess Elfgifa some time after her arrival on the Continent renounced her original name and its continental abbreviation and accepted the name of Emma. We know her by this name from the Chronicle of Cosmas and from the Wolfenbüttel Codex and this is the name she used on her own coins.

The marriage of an Anglo-Saxon princess to a member of the Přemysl dynasty was undoubtedly of importance for the Czech State. It is even possible that the name of the owner of the manor of Laverstoke, spelt Ulveva Beteslau in Domesday Book, which has puzzled whole generations of English scholars, is the corrupted form of Alveva (Elfgifa) Boleslavi and signifies the life-rent dowry of the princess.

In the early 11th century the Czech State consisted practically of Bohemia alone. The Přemysl rulers of Bohemia, i.e. the descendants of the mythical Přemysl the Ploughman and his wife, the prophetess and Princess Libuše, had to unite the different tribes occupying Bohemia and Moravia. The Slavonic inhabitants of present-day Slovakia were incorporated into the Kingdom of Hungary and remained in that realm until 1918.

In the Middle Ages, both kings and Church were important forces. We see the efficiency of Church organisation in the rapidity with which information spread through Europe. Before Henry II, the great Plantagenet king, started his feud against the Emperor, he sent him a crown, with which King Vladislav I was crowned in 1158. Vladislav was one of those ambitious rulers of Bohemia whose help was essential to the Emperors for their foreign policy, and who did their best to strengthen their position against the Empire. After the same Henry II gave orders to murder Thomas Becket, the monks of the monastery of Milevsko in Southern Bohemia were well informed of the matter, stating in their chronicle that the deeds of the Canterbury martyr were well known to them.

Apart from Thomas of Canterbury, St. George, the patron saint of England, had been immensely popular in Bohemia from time immemorial. The oldest churches and monasteries bore his name and for centuries his statue has adorned Prague Castle. St. George's Cross became the flag of England during the reign of Richard I, the Lionhearted, romantic crusader and prisoner of the Emperor, that same Emperor who deposed Prince Přemysl Otakar I of Bohemia in 1193, because of his contacts with the hated Englishman. Four years later Richard was free and Přemysl became King of Bohemia.

Among Přemysl's most faithful followers and probably a friend of his ever since his forced exile in Germany was an English Cistercian monk, known in Bohemia as Robert the Englishman. Robert, a native of Herefordshire, spent nearly forty years in Central Europe. His activities as one of the directors of the royal chancery (the famous "dictator", i.e. Chancellor Otakarus 5, is almost certainly identical with Robert) and as Bishop of Moravia are documented from 1200 to his death some time about 1240. Robert was certainly a "political" bishop, sent by his royal master to Moravia to complete the union of this land with Bohemia. He was also a gifted man of letters. His commentary to the *Song of Solomon* reveals him as a twelfth-century "humanist", who knew Greek and perhaps Hebrew, and had probably read both *De natura amoris* of his fellow-Cistercian Guillaume de Saint-Thierry and Ovid's *Ars amandi*. This unusual bishop was a relentless fighter against irrationalism and mysticism and was courageous enough to side with his royal friend against the Papacy. No wonder that he was summoned to Rome three times and died probably on the verge of excommunication. He knew a great deal about the splendid legacy of the Great Moravian Empire and was, according to tradition, buried in the monastery of Velehrad, which he had founded and called after the half-mythical capital of Great Moravia.

Moreover, Robert the Englishman was a practical man and proceeded with colonising work, traditionally but wrongly attributed to one of his successors, Bishop Bruno. In these activities he found an outstanding helper in Arnold de Hogenswag (or Hucesvage) a member of the mission sent to Bohemia in 1228 by the English King Henry III. At that time, the idea of a marriage between Princess Agnes, daughter of King Přemysl I, and Henry III was discussed. Somehow the project failed, Princess Agnes remained unmarried and built in the Old Town of Prague a beautiful cloister, parts of which today house a museum of early Gothic art. The name of Arnold de Hucesvage is connected with the settlement of the Moravian borderland against Poland and Hungary, including the town of Ostrava, today the centre of an important industrial region.

Přemysl I's successor, King Wenceslas I, was mentioned in the chronicle of Matthew of Paris for his defence against the Tartar invasion in the 13th century. The great advance of the Mongol people from China and Central Asia westwards across the steppes of Russia into Hungary, Poland, Silesia and Moravia, revealed once more the importance of the medieval Kingdom of Bohemia. William Rishanger's chronicle contains a brief account of the ambitious foreign policy of King Přemysl Otakar II, grandson of Přemysl I, who was for a decade an ally of Richard of Cornwall, Emperor-

The first English map of Bohemia, the work of John Speed, 1626

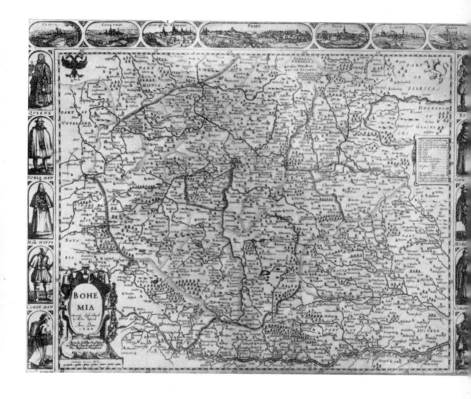

Ruins of Devín Castle, one of the centres
of the Great Moravian Empire (9th century).

The *denarii* of Anglo-Saxon type struck
by the rulers of 10th-11th-century Bohemia.

The statue of "Good King Wenceslas"
in St. Guy's Cathedral, Prague.

Hukvaldy, the Castle of Arnold de Hucesvage,
who came to Bohemia in 1228 as a member
of a mission sent by England's King Henry III.

Part of the Romanesque Castle Palace at Olomouc,
the residence of Bishop Robert
the Englishman in the early 13th century.

Princess Anne, Charles IV's daughter,
became the Good Queen of England after her marriage to Richard II.
(From a print by W. Hollar.)

The bust of Charles IV (1316—78),
King of Bohemia and Emperor of the Holy Roman Empire,
in the St. Guy triforium.

John Wyclif and John Hus
from a 16th-century Czech manuscript.

Portrait of Edmund Campion
in Prague's Clementine College.

St. Thomas's in the Little Quarter of Prague
is the burying place of Jane Elizabeth Weston
(1582—1612), poetess.
Her tombstone is the first on the left.

Karlštejn Castle,
founded by Charles IV in 1348 and defended
by an Anglo-Scottish regiment in 1620.

Elect, from whom he obtained an important charter in 1262. For a time, his dominions spread from the Bohemian Mountains almost to the Adriatic coast. And the son of a Czech knight, Orderic of Pordenone, explored in the days of Marco Polo the mysterious East as far as Malaysia and Indonesia and southern China. But the grandiose conception of Přemysl II was frustrated when the Papal Curia put a stop to the plans of his successor, King Wenceslas II. In 1302 Wenceslas sent a mission to England, which is credited with bringing back to Prague the relics of Thomas of Canterbury to the new church, then being built in the Lesser Town of Prague.

Most 13th-century English chronicles contain brief descriptions of Bohemia; that by John Trevisa is especially charming: "Bohemia is closed almost all about with hills and woods, and has great plenty of pastures, and of grass that smells full sweet..." Pastoral Bohemia sent her King, John of Luxemburg, to his death while fighting against the English army under the Black Prince in the battle of Crécy (1346). Laurence Minot in an almost contemporary poem on the battle, refers to the King of "Beme" (Bohemia) as "cant and kene". The antiquarian William Camden retold the story in his *Remains* at the beginning of the 17th century and Ben Jonson composed a short poem on the fatal battle:

(The Black Prince Edward at Cressy field)... teares
From the Bohemian crown the plume he weares,
Which after for his creste he did preserve
To his father's use, with this fit word, *I serve*.

It is not quite certain that the motto is really of Bohemian origin and the historian is rather surprised by the change of the eagle feathers, used by King John on his crest, into the unusual ostrich feathers. King John's son, Charles, who was wounded at Crécy, as Emperor Charles IV nearly married the English Princess Isabella and, on 23rd April 1348, the year in which he founded Prague University, he concluded the first pact of alliance between the two countries.

But even in the 14th century, international relations did not depend on kings, princesses and clerics alone. In the 'fifties, a group of miners from Bohemia was invited to England. Bohemia, of course, was then one of the richest countries in deposits of silver-ore, and her miners were welcome helpers in 16th-century England, too. The Caroline (or Great) College of Prague soon entered into relations with the leading universities of the West, the Sorbonne, Bologna, and also with Oxford and Cambridge.

While these cultural contacts were spreading, another princess entered the field of dynastic policy. Princess Anne, the daughter of Charles IV and the sister of his son and successor, Wenceslas IV, became the queen of young Richard II. The Crown Archives, now a part of the Central State Archives of Prague, still preserve the marriage contract made at Westminster. Although "Good Queen Anne" died young, she has left permanent traces in English literature and created another important link between the England of Wyclif and the Bohemia of John Hus. Chaucer's *House of Fame* is traditionally associated with her wedding, *The Legend of Good Women* contains a direct appeal to her, while *The Parliament of Fowls* is, according to some authorities, reflected in the Czech *Council of Animals*, written by the nobleman Smil Flaška of Pardubice. The superb Middle English poem *Pearl* may not have anything in common with Bohemia, but its theme reappears in the German version, written in Bohemia and called *The Ploughman and Death*. The Czech version, *Tkadleček*, is a tragi-comical treatment of the same theme, the bereavement of the lover. Gower's *Confessio Amantis* speaks of the "new guise of Beaume" — a new fashion from Bohemia. But almost certainly the poet was alluding to pointed caps of French, not Bohemian origin. Old English chronicles contain scandalous stories concerning one of the Good Queen's ladies-in-waiting. The frivolous "Lancecrona", married to Robert de Vere and heroine of these scandals (they even called her a "filia ignobilis"), had probably nothing to do with the honest East-Bohemian town of Lanškroun. She was, it seems, a member of the noble family of the lords of Krajíř, owners of the castle of Landštejn in the Bohemian-Moravian borderland. At least we know that one of them participated in the mission to England in 1381. But soon after Anne's death, which, as we are told, left the King prostrate, another type of contact overshadowed that of court intrigues.

The Peasants' Rising of 1381 left undeniable traces in the work and life of all its contemporaries and was a picture of things to come in far-away Bohemia.

2

The lively contacts between England and Bohemia during the Hussite period have been widely discussed both in Czech and in English literature. The late Professor G. M. Trevelyan stressed the influence of Wyclif and the Lollards on Bohemia, always open to religious reformers. His younger colleague, the late Professor R. R. Betts, pointed out that the social basis of the two movements, Lollardism and Hussitism, when rationally analysed, explain why so many of the Wyclifite articles were included in the Hussite programme. Czech students had been coming to England from the middle of the 14th century. The learned Professor Adalbert Ranconis de Ericinio was one of the first, and he founded a scholarship for Prague students travelling to the Sorbonne or to Oxford. Master Jerome of Prague, a friend and fellow-martyr of John Hus, was in England before 1401 and two Prague students brought copies of Wyclif's work to Prague in 1406 or 1407. In those years a discussion regarding Wyclif's teaching was already in full swing at the faculties of the Caroline University of Prague, the Czech masters defending their Oxford colleague, the German masters usually condemning him just as vehemently. Letters were exchanged between the English Lollards, R. Wyche and Sir John Oldcastle, and John Hus, King Wenceslas and some Hussite noblemen in Bohemia. When Hus was martyred at Constance in 1415, the Czech noblemen protested and one of these protests found its way to the University Library of Edinburgh.

Another "forgotten great Englishman" found in Hussite Bohemia not only a refuge, but also a responsive public. He was Peter Payne (Engliš, as he was called in Bohemia, i.e. the Englishman), an Oxford Master of Arts, Principal of St. Edmund's Hall and the head of the Lollard Masters until his departure for Prague where he was to forge a link between England and Bohemia. He brought with him several books written by John Wyclif and treating of the remanence of the substance of the bread and wine in the consecrated elements. Thus he helped to establish in Hussite Bohemia the doctrine of communion for the laity in both kinds at a time when the Chalice was becoming the symbol of the Hussite Revolution. In 1417 Payne became a Master of the University of Prague and was soon one of its representative debaters. As a diplomat of Hussite Bohemia he defended the articles condemning the temporal power and wealth of the Church. He was the outspoken defender of the Hussite programme at Kutná Hora (1421), Cracow (1421 and 1431), at Bratislava (1429) and at Basle (1432). During his missions to Poland, he showed great understanding for the common interests of the Czech and Polish nations.

Peter Payne was one of the members of the Hussite Consistory, belonging to the "centre" of the movement before 1434. After the defeat of the radical wing at Lipany (1434) he became one of the most esteemed representatives of the Taborite "radicals". In the forties he seems to have left Bohemia for the Principality of Moldavia in present-day Rumania. In 1452 he led a mission sent by the Hussite Church to Constantinople, and spent the last years of his life in the "Slavonic Monastery" of Prague, in close contact with the head of the Hussite Church, the Archbishop-elect John Rokycana, and Brother Řehoř (Gregory), one of the founders of the famous Unity of Brethren. The frustrated stirrings of fifteenth-century Bohemia won at least a partial victory in seventeenth-century England, but Peter Payne, connecting in his own person and wanderings Britain and Bohemia, still has a message to carry to the people of today.

Yet Hussite Bohemia was generally considered a dangerous seat of religious and social heresy throughout Europe, and 15th-century England proved no exception. The English Master John Stokes debated with Hus in Prague in 1412, and Emperor Sigismund, refused as King by his Czech subjects, was well accepted in England in 1416, when he concluded a pact with Henry V at Canterbury. In 1417 Sir John Oldcastle paid the penalty as a rebel in much the same way as John Hus and Jerome of Prague. A prince of the royal house, Henry of Beaufort, Bishop of Winchester, even headed an unsuccessful crusade against the Hussites.

As the Lollard movement was crushed and had to go underground, we have few favourable English comments on Bohemia from 1417 on. On the contrary, Hussite Bohemia, like so many revolutionary countries, was ostracized and held up as a warning to the faithful. Reginald Pecock in his *Repressor of Over Much Blaming of the Clergy* (1449) speaks of the evils brought on by the Hussite wars. Sir John Fortescue in his *Governance of England* (1471–6) sees Bohemia's fate as an example of where anarchy leads, Alexander Barclay links "those of Boeme" with barbarous Scythians (*The Ship of Fools*, 1509) and John Skelton couples the "Hussians" with "Wycliffista, the devilish dogmatista" in his *Colyn Clout* (1522).

The only relatively positive appraisal of Bohemia is to be found in the chronicle written before 1470 by John Capgrave. For the first time in English literature he told the charming story of St. Wenceslas, "how Wenceslas used to rise secretly at night and go, with only one slave attending him, to his forest, and bearing wood thence on his shoulders, he used to lay it secretly at the doors of widows and poor people. He also used to collect corn in his field, and secretly tearing off the stalks and making wafers with his own hand, he distributed them among the churches".

Peter Payne's manuscript
list of Wyclif's writings.

A clearer picture of England was left to future generations of Czech readers by another Wenceslas, Václav Šašek of Bířkov, member of a diplomatic mission sent to Western Europe by King George of Bohemia, and led by his Catholic brother-in law, Zdeněk Lev of Rožmitál. Šašek's charming travel book gives a vivid account of the English court in 1465, describing many personalities known from Shakespeare's *Richard III*, stressing inevitably such aspects of English life as were alien to contemporary Bohemia: the sea and the ships, different manners and ways. On the whole, the Czechs thought much better of England than the English thought of Bohemia. There were no English travellers to leave us a description of the land of the heretics. The main source of information used to be the Latin *Chronicle of Bohemia* written by the Italian Humanist Aeneas Silvius Piccolomini, long before he became Pope under the name of Pius II. It was Aeneas Silvius who made the serious mistake of identifying the Adamites, a Chiliast or Adventist sect, who were destroyed by the Hussites, with the Hussites themselves, and thus perpetuating the idea among learned readers up to the 18th century that Bohemia was a precursor of the nudist movement. Another little work of Aeneas Silvius, his *Godly History of the Lady Lucres: alias The History of the Amours of Count Schlick* narrating the amorous adventures of a Bohemian nobleman, was published in 1550 and many times reissued. Thus, at a time when Bohemia was struggling for an ideal of religious tolerance and social justice, her name was acquiring that aura of disorder, sedition and romanticism, which under the influence of French terminology, it has retained to this day.

When the Reformation came to England, Bohemia and Czech Hussitism again became burning questions for Englishmen. We are told that Henry VIII received his title, Defender of the Faith, from the Pope in 1521 as a reward for his early pamphlet attacking Martin Luther and the Hussites. His Lord Chancellor, Sir Thomas More, the author of *Utopia*, was astonished by the obvious religious tolerance in Bohemia and did not feel inclined to welcome it. And, if we may believe the biographer of Cardinal Wolsey, even he was thinking of the Bohemian heretics and mentioned Bohemia as a warning to Henry VIII in a message from his death-bed. But, in spite of all these warnings, the Reformation from above was carried out in England, in contrast to the popular reform movement in Hussite Bohemia.

We know today that one of the first English reformers, Leonard Coxe, spent several years teaching at municipal grammar schools in the Slovak towns of Levoča (1520-1) and Košice, protected probably by Queen Mary of Hungary, the wife of the last King of the Jagellon dynasty, Louis, who lost his life in 1526 while fighting the Turks at Mohács. After this date, Mary's brother Ferdinand I became King of Bohemia and Hungary. His European policy clashed with the "balance of power", envisaged by Henry VIII, in so far as the latter threatened the political interests of Emperor Charles V, brother of Ferdinand and Mary. Bohemia, Moravia and Upper Hungary (today Slovakia), from 1526 parts of the multi-national monarchy of the Austrian Habsburgs, had to finance the ambitious policy of the House of Austria, both on its Eastern front against the Turks and on the Western front in the struggle for the Atlantic. But Queen Mary, until the fifties the Lieutenant-General of her imperial brother in the Netherlands, never lost financial and social contacts with England, and her court at Brussels was the best clearing-house for England for many visitors from Central Europe.

Among these were, once again, noblemen, miners and students.

Owing to the "official" character of the English Reformation, no change of attitude towards Hussite Bohemia occurred before the short period of persecution during the reign of Queen Mary. The turning point in Anglo-Czech relations is therefore 1554, when John Foxe published his *Acts and Monuments*, containing the famous "History of Master John Hus". From then on, there are frequent references to Hus, Jerome of Prague and Hussitism in Protestant literature, and the despised herectic was now acclaimed as a revered member of the new Protestant hagiography, which cherished the relation of Hus's "most cruel death and martyrdom for the testimony of the truth of our Lord Jesus Christ". In Scotland in the reign of Mary Stuart, John Knox revered in a similar way another Hussite heretic, Master Pavel Kravař, called Paul Crawar or Craw, burned at the stake in St. Andrews in 1433.

3

Between the middle of the sixteenth century and the end of the English Commonwealth in 1660 a revolutionary transformation took place in Europe. Two conceptions of civilisation were in conflict. One took the Spanish Monarchy as its model, the other the Dutch Republic, which had arisen from the struggle of the rebellious bourgeoisie. In the end, neither of these models prevailed: it was England and France that set the examples on the path of economic advance, modern types of government and of scientific and cultural progress.

It is remarkable that in this period British-Czech relations first reached a culmination.

For most readers this will probably mean the old problem of the sea-coast of Bohemia in Shakespeare's *Winter's Tale*. What could be further from the reality of Bohemia than Antigonus' question to the Mariner:

"Thou art perfect, then, our ship hath touch'd upon
The deserts of Bohemia?"

It is not so important to know how much Shakespeare knew of Bohemia when he was writing his play, for this tale of the breakdown and reconstruction of the most intimate human bonds is a piece of symbolism, of subtle poetic imagery, where Sicily (or perhaps Sysyly-Silesia) and Bohemia are clearly countries of the imagination. Thus *The Winter's Tale* and its setting say nothing about Shakespeare's knowledge of geography and are no criterion of the intensity of cultural relations existing between the two countries. Nor is the fact that Shakespeare's plays were possibly performed in Bohemia and Moravia by the actors of the Greene-Browne company in 1617. They almost certainly came to these lands at this time and again in the winter of 1619-20, but their performances could, for social and linguistic reasons, have had only a limited audience. Knowledge of Shakespeare's plays is not conclusively evidenced until later in the 17th century.

In Shakespeare's time Bohemia and Moravia were often visited by renowned Englishmen. For instance, Sir Philip Sidney paid several visits to Prague where, in 1577, he tried in vain to win Rudolf II for the Anti-Spanish League. Edmund Campion spent five years in Prague as a lecturer in rhetorics at the Jesuit St. Clement's College (1574-9), and his drama *Saul* was very probably produced here by his pupils. Fynes Moryson gave a description of both the Utraquist and the Catholic university college, and left behind a valuable account of plays performed in Prague at Easter-tide, 1592. But Campion's work is by far the most important, because, although the plot was based on the Bible, its appeal was political, being an indirect attack on Queen Elizabeth.

St. Thomas' in Prague is the burying place of Elizabeth Jane Weston (1582-1612), who came to Bohemia early in her life with her father and made her home in Prague. She was educated by another émigré, the humanist Hammon, and had for her stepfather Edward Kelley-Talbot. Kelley was a remarkable natural philosopher as well as a secret agent, and provided the model for Ben Jonson's *Alchemist*. Miss Weston, or Vestonia, as she was called in Bohemia, soon excelled by her learning and her Latin poems. She was praised for her facility in Latin, Italian, Czech and German and has remained one of the outstanding writers of humanist Latin verse.

There were virtually dozens of visitors from Bohemia and Moravia to Great Britain in Queen Elizabeth's time and during the reign of James I. One of the leaders of the Utraquist University in the stormy years of the anti-Habsburg Rising (1618-20), Master Peter Fradelius, born in Banská Štiavnica in Slovakia, spent a short time in England in 1617 and even dedicated one of his writings to James I. He was also responsible for the publications offered by the University in 1619-1620 to the King-Elect Frederick of the Palatinate and his Stuart Queen Elizabeth. The first Czech visitor to England who saw a play at The Globe in July 1600 was a young Moravian nobleman, Zdeněk Brtnický of Valdštejn, a distant relative of the more famous Albert of Wallenstein. He left a description of it in his *Iter in Angliam:* "We have heard an English comedy. The theatre has been built in the style of ancient Roman theatres and made of beams in such a way that from all sides the audience can easily see all the details of the play". He did not comment on the play itself, as he had not sufficient knowledge of English. But he saw quite a lot of England, noticed her mighty fleet, always fascinating to continental visitors, and the wealth of the bourgeoisie, especially in London. He even found time to visit Richmond, the royal castle where the Good Queen Anne of Bohemia had died. In Zdeněk's diary we read that "she was the first to teach the English ladies the refinement of manners which is now so common in England".

Among the political and social problems seen in Shakespeare's plays, some were common to contemporary England and Bohemia. Shakespeare was a strong believer in monarchy, defending England against a foreign (Spanish) invasion and internal anarchy. The solution of social conflicts, conventionally expressed as a conflict between Court and Country, as seen in *The Winter's Tale*, is, of course, quite unrealistic. Only in a fairy-tale manner was it possible to reconcile the conflicts which shook Bohemia shortly after 1618 and England only twenty years later.

Along with the Bohemia of the sea-coast, the historical Bohemia, a small but noteworthy country in the heart of the Continent, found its place in Elizabethan fiction and drama. Thomas Lodge knew the old tales about Valasca (Vlasta) and the Women's Revolt, but he also knew Bohemia's true geographical situation. Despite this it was above all "The Bohemian historie written by Pope Pius" and other Italian Renaissance sources — all of them hostile towards Hussite Bohemia — that served to supply information to Elizabethan and Jacobean novelists and dramatists, to Painter, Whetstone, Marlowe, Greene, Dekker, Shakespeare and Jonson. Only at the very beginning of the 17th century did England display an interest in Bohemia for political and religious reasons. A number of eminent diplomats came to Prague, while English publicists like Brerewood emphasized the importance of Bohemia for plans directed against the Spanish and Austrian Habsburgs. In Bohemia, too, we find a heightening of interest in England. But in 1618 the number of men well versed in Central European problems was exceedingly small, and many of them were excluded from political activity during the crucial period.

The Winter's Tale was performed at the wedding of Princess Elizabeth, the daughter of James I, to Frederick Count Palatine in 1613. In 1619 Frederick ascended the throne of Bohemia, then in open struggle against the Habsburgs. The Bohemian Estates were expecting substantial aid from their potential allies: the German Protestants, the Netherlands, England, perhaps even from Venice and the Swiss. But James I, "the wisest fool in Christendom", was far from becoming a member of such a dangerous coalition.

THE
historie
of
BOHEMIA.

THE FIRST PARTE.

describing

THE COVNTRYE SCITVATI= on, climate, commodities,

the name and nature of the people

AND COMPENDIOVSLY CONTINVĪG

the Historie from the begining of
the Nation to their first
Christian Prince a=
bout the yeare of

Christ
990

The title page
of *The Historie
of Bohemia*, 1619–20,
probably
by John Harrison.

He did not like the rebellious Dutch and he did not wish to become an ally of the even more rebellious Bohemian Estates. We shall not discuss the policy of James, the "Peacemaker", recorded in pamphlets and correspondence. Thanks to this "first Czech crisis", the real Bohemia was brought to the notice of Englishmen. At this time an anonymous author, probably John Harrison, a groom to Princess Elizabeth, compiled the first English history of Bohemia. Here are some quotations from it:

"Bohemia is one of the richest, civilest and strongest nations of Europe... It has had more wars with the Pope and won more victories against him, and his partakers than any other nation. (The Bohemians) kept the faith in Christ better and purer than any other nation; they have stoutly defended it and many of them died for it; they maintained it against the Pope; and all the Kings of Europe who were then the slaves to the Pope and not one of them so free as the king of Bohemia".

John Taylor, the Water Poet, wished much success to his countrymen who were leaving England to fight for the unhappy Winter Queen (*An Englishman's Love to Bohemia: with a friendly farewell to all the noble souldiers that goe from Great Britain to that honorable expedition*. 1620). His interest in the Bohemian cause was so great that he set out from London and travelled to Prague in the late summer of 1620. After his return he published *Taylor his Travels: from the City of London in England, to the City of Prague in Bohemia*, with an interesting picture of the Bohemian capital:

"Prague is a famous, ancient, kingly seat,
In situation and in state complete,
In Architecture stately: in Attire

Bezonians and Plebeians do aspire,
To be apparell'd with the stately port
Of worship, honor, or the royal court..."

While companies of volunteers were leaving England, James was sending one mission after another to the Continent. One of the ill-fated diplomats, the poet Sir Henry Wotton, wrote his famous poem *On His Mistress, the Queen of Bohemia*, in Greenwich Park just before he set out. Although the sympathies of most Englishmen were on the side of the Bohemians, James's attitude remained lukewarm at best. In truth, the Court of St. James secretly negotiated with the Spanish ambassador in the summer of 1620 and offered not only to abandon Bohemia but to attack the United Provinces of the Netherlands. Thus an Irish chaplain in the Imperial army, Henry Fitzsimon, and the English secretary to the Queen, Sir Francis Nethersole, were the only witnesses of the final Bohemian collapse, during which an Anglo-Scottish infantry regiment tried in vain to hold the Castle of Karlštejn. That was the end of old Bohemia.

When the news of the Battle of the White Mountain, of the "disaster in Bohemia" reached London, James's reaction was to dispatch two more missions — one to Frederick to tell him to give up the fight, and the other to the Emperor to persuade him to withdraw from the Palatinate. Public opinion reacted more simply and unambiguously by staging wild anti-Spanish demonstrations. In December, 1620, James had to give way to public pressure by consenting to summon Parliament. On the other hand, he persecuted the authors of satirical pamphlets who favoured the "Bohemian cause", which became one of the most serious problems of European politics. It had its significance for England, too, since the attitude towards Bohemia made manifest the absolute division between King James I with the small pro-Spanish court faction, as against the overwhelming majority of his subjects. After the convening of Parliament the discussion on foreign policy reached such heights of criticism that James knew no other means to silence the critics than to dissolve Parliament. Thus in 1621 the Bohemian cause made radical opposition to the régime possible.

After 1621 interest in Bohemia declined but individual members of the opposition established relations with some dispersed groups of Bohemian exiles. John Speed, in his *Prospect of the Most Famous Parts of the World* (published in 1631), placed Bohemia and Moravia only after Greece, the Roman Empire and Germany. Robert Burton, author of *The Anatomy of Melancholy* (1621), and Izaak Walton, in his *Compleat Angler* (1653), were well aware of the economic importance of Bohemia. Herbert of Cherbury, a partisan of the Bohemian cause in 1620, praised the wisdom of the Czech educationalist John Amos Comenius in his *Autobiography*. The English admirers of Comenius, the "Comenians", published his works in England from the thirties. They included such eminent members of the opposition as John Pym. In 1641, when Comenius came to England at the invitation of this group, Parliament debated the destiny of the Palatine's family, but in the debates of the Long Parliament problems of foreign policy were soon overshadowed by problems of domestic concern. The circle of Comenius' friends broke up in the years 1641–2, when those of its members from the high nobility and ecclesiastical hierarchy came into conflict with members of the gentry and bourgeoisie who stood firmly by Parliment.

The representative *History of the Persecutions of the Bohemian Church*, a work in which Comenius had also collaborated, was published at the height of the revolution to serve the political purposes of the Independents, whom Comenius, however, criticized at about the same time. It is worth mentioning that the English radicals at this time used even older Hussite works to serve their cause. William Prynne printed in 1641 *A reasonable vindication of the supreme authority and jurisdiction of Christian kings, Lords, Parliaments, as well over the possessions or the persons of delinquent prelates and churchmen; or an antient Disputation of the famous Bohemian Martyr John Huss...* "to subjoin some memorable domestick evidences and precedents in all eyes to justifie their opinions in point of practice". Another case where Hus's arguments were used against high churchmen occurred in a booklet, published in 1649 under the title: *The City-ministers unmasked — A vindication of the Ministers of the Gospel in and about the City of London. Together with a prophecie of John Hus...*

While the Bohemian rebels were implicitly friends of revolutionary England, the Habsburgs ranked among their inveterate enemies. Only Catholic Irishmen and Scots could achieve a career in a Catholic Bohemia deprived of its nobility. Among those who planned and performed the murder of Wallenstein at Cheb (Eger) in 1634 we find: Colonel Walter Butler, Lieutenant-Colonel John Gordon, supposed to be one of the ancestors of the poet Lord Byron, Captains Walter Devereux and Walter Leslie and the chaplain Patrick Taaffe. In 1631, the Hybernian monastery was founded in Prague for Irish monks. *Albertus Wallenstein*, a highly fantastic drama by Henry Glapthorne, produced in 1639, is evidence of surviving interest in Bohemian matters.

One of the men who helped to overthrow Wallenstein and who became his successor and lieutenant-general of the Spanish Netherlands, Ottavio Piccolomini, helps to clarify the attitude of the Habsburgs and their representatives towards revolutionary England.

From the letters Piccolomini exchanged between 1642 and 1649 with his agents — all of whom were English royalists — we see that the Habsburg policy was determined by two contradictory motives. On the one hand the Spaniards (as well as the French court who opposed them) favoured the cause of the English and Irish royalists, but on the other hand they wanted to fill the thinning ranks of their armies on the battlefields with mercenaries from England and Ireland. In the interval between the First and the Second Civil War, notably in 1647, a tacit agreement seems to have been reached between the Spanish commanders in the Netherlands and Charles I, implying that royalist regiments in Spanish service would be at his disposal in case of further struggle against Parliament. The events of 1648, however, showed that neither France nor Spain placed the interests of the English monarchy above their own. In supporting the royalist attack against Scotland the leading part was played by the rulers of the United Netherlands.

At the beginning of the Thirty Years' War as at its end, the Habsburgs and the English friends of defeated Bohemia found themselves in the rival political camps into which Europe was divided at that time. The policy of the Habsburgs was hostile to the anti-Stuart opposition and later to revolutionary England. The spokesmen of the Bohemian emigrants, led by Comenius, looked upon England as their natural ally and protector. Cromwell's Commonwealth invited them to settle down in Ireland, after the town of Leszno (Lissa) in Poland had been destroyed, and the Lord Protector himself spoke sharply against Habsburg policies in 1658. But even then the emigrants did not give up all their hopes and the offer was never seriously considered. In 1659, towards the close of the Commonwealth period, the Bohemian War (1618-20) found its first English historian in John Rushworth.

Significantly, Rushworth's *Historical Collections* was primarily a justification of the English Revolution. According to Rushworth, a contributory cause of the English Civil War was dissatisfaction with the foreign policy of James I over the question of Bohemia; therefore he designated the year 1618 as the beginning of the struggle between the Crown and the "people of England". From a more global viewpoint the Bohemian War and the subsequent struggle for the "Bohemian cause" appeared and still appear as one act in the great conflict of two conceptions of civilisation. In this conflict the Czechs fought for the further existence of their social system, as it had been formed in the main during the Hussite wars, for the ideal of a representative monarchy against absolutism, for a society based on the Estates as against a revived feudalism, for religious tolerance against dogmatic bigotry. Seen by an English observer, the struggle in the centre of the Continent falls into line with the general conflict between the monarchs and the new elements of society. For a little while Britain and Bohemia stood side by side, although the progress of events was to divide them so soon and so decisively.

4

During the seventeenth century modern English society and the modern state began to take shape. The England of Elizabeth I was still a second-class power, the Great Britain of one century later was the greatest power in the world. During the eighteenth century she lost her first colonial empire and built up another, and colonial questions dominated British policy-making. We can say, with some simplification, that the seventeenth century set England on the path of Parliamentary government, economic advance, imperialist foreign policy and scientific progress. Two centuries after Comenius had failed to be impressed by his visit to England, his countrymen saw in England a great teacher, a model and a threat.

The object of this chapter is to throw some light on the changes which occurred in the relations between Britain and the Central European peoples living in Bohemia, Moravia and Slovakia. The traditional account of their complete decline in this new "Dark Age" is only partially correct. It is true, of course, that between the middle of the 17th and the middle of the 19th century the countries of Central Europe were economically subordinate to the countries of Western Europe.

Undoubtedly there was a regress in the economy, standard of living, cultural level, and the consequences of the Thirty Years' War and, above all, the new lease of life given to feudalism in the Habsburg state, imposed a heavy burden. The peasants were oppressed and exploited by a new land-owning oligarchy and their exploitation shocked visitors from the West. Charles Patin, whose *Travels through Germany, Bohemia... and other Parts of Europe* were published in London in 1697, was not exaggerating when he described the poverty of the peasants, crushed after their savage revolt of 1680, and the splendour of their master's castles and palaces.

Nevertheless, the first steps towards capitalist industrial development were being taken in Bohemia. Soon after the war voices were heard pointing out that Central Europe should follow the example of the Netherlands, France and England. As early as 1653 P. I. Morgenthaler, a burgher of Brno, in Moravia, requested the Emperor to allow artisans to be brought into the country to produce goods hitherto purchased abroad. Ten years later another Moravian, F. S. Malivský, advocated building manufactories.

The first manufactories followed traditional lines. Before the Thirty Years' War Bohemia and Moravia had been renowned for their excellent linen goods. Big German commercial houses used to conclude collective agreements with local craft guilds. After the war the centre of production shifted to the countryside. Soon there appeared small country traders or factors, who bought up the products of the country spinners and weavers and resold them to the big foreign trading firms. From the end of the 16th century there were even some Dutchmen and Englishmen among these, but the English were still mainly preoccupied with the import of cloth. At least that seems to have been the main interest of a Mr. Farringdon, who lived in Prague before 1618. In the second half of the seventeenth century, English capital began to penetrate into the Bohemian linen industry, directly and indirectly. Through factors and head-factors, Bohemian and Moravian linen reached Leipzig and Hamburg, was shipped to London, and probably re-exported to America and other British dependencies. It can be said that, from the end of the 17th century, the putting-out system in Northern Bohemia, Moravia and Silesia was responsible for a large part of the linen imported by England. Bohemian Glass, too, found its way to England. Since the glassmakers and refiners sold their products themselves, we can follow their activities on the Continent, and especially in the privileged markets of the Spanish and British colonies. In the latter half of the eighteenth century this was one of the ways the inhabitants of Bohemia learned about the struggle of the colonies against the metropolitan countries.

By the beginning of the eighteenth century, English merchant-enterpreneurs had begun to settle in Bohemia. One of them, Robert Allason, set up his enterprise in the North-Bohemian town of Rumburk in 1713. Through his factors he employed hundreds of country spinners and weavers and exported linen goods up to an annual turnover of nearly half a million gulden. Some aristocrats followed Allason's example, especially those who, like Count F. J. Kinský, came to England on diplomatic missions. Kennedy Wellens wrote to Count Rudolph Chotek that Bohemian linen was exported in 1756 as far as Philadelphia and New York. English specialists were invited to the woollen manufactory at Horní Litvínov, the property of Count Waldstein, who had big English-style presses made for it. The *Designatio Iconographica* of 1728 depicts this important manufacturing centre.

During the struggle of the French, at that time another manufacturing power, against the Dutch United Provinces, both England and the Habsburg Emperor opposed France. Official relations between Great Britain and the Emperor were maintained by diplomats, who had estates in Bohemia and Moravia. Exceptionally, they brought brief descriptions of England; from time to time, as we have already seen, they came back with new economic ideas. Some of these Austrian ambassadors were remarkable people, among them the trusted collaborator of Prince Eugene of Savoy and the Duke of Marlborough, Wenceslas Wratislav of Mitrovice, the Supreme

Chancellor during the difficult years of the War of the Spanish Succession, and his successor as envoy to the Court of St. James, John Wenceslas Count Gallas, who was expelled rather unceremoniously because of an indiscretion, by the express order of Queen Anne. Before his departure, he published in London, in 1706, *A Memorial Presented to Her Britannick Majesty* on two projects: "The first contains the project to open a Passage for the Trade of the English Nation to the Levant, thro' the Territories of His Imperial Majesty, by the means of the Rivers Elbe, Oder and Danube..." The second concerned the "Demand of a Loan, sufficient to remedy the Disorder of the Imperial Treasury", caused by the civil war in Hungary.

Wratislav and Gallas had no easy task in trying to get subsidies from the unwilling ally for the "disordered treasury" and to secure the cooperation of Marlborough's army on the Rhine with the troops of Prince Eugene. The project of building a canal connecting the Elbe, the Oder and the Danube via Wroclaw and Bratislava has remained on paper to this day, and, in general, all the loans the English eventually gave to the Emperor had to be guaranteed by the Bohemian or Silesian Estates, since the countries of the old Bohemian Crown were rich and their people industrious, while the Emperors were poor and ambitious. Another project which has remained on paper was an Austro-British condominium of the Spanish West Indies, also suggested to the English by the prolific Gallas. His successors were even less successful and, under British and Dutch pressure, had to give their consent to the closure of the India Company, founded under the auspices of Prince Eugene at Ostend.

During the War of the Spanish Succession, while Britain was already an ally of the Austrian Habsburgs, the old tradition of

Protestant Bohemia showed the last signs of vitality. From the seventeenth century the Church of England, and especially some of its institutions, had given wholehearted support to the "afflicted Protestants" of Bohemia, Moravia and Hungary. The Sion College of London has a wonderful collection of older Czech literature on the "Bohemian cause". The old and revered Queen of Bohemia died in 1662, and her son, Prince Rupert, "Duke of Lusatia", born in Prague in December, 1619, was not much interested in his native land. The old émigrés were dying, among them Wenceslas Hollar, the famous artist and engraver, who did so much to preserve the memory of old London. He was buried at St. Margaret's Church, Westminster in 1677.

Nevertheless, Bohemia was not completely forgotten. The Hartmanns, a Bohemian family, had close connections with Christ Church, Oxford. Adam Samuel Hartmann even prevailed on Archbishop William Sancroft to offer scholarships to the progeny of the Bohemian exiles (1679). Among the scholars was the grandson of Comenius, Daniel Ernest Jablonský (1660-1741), whose older friends were John Fell, John Pococke and the Bishop of London, Henry Compton. After studying in London in the turbulent years 1680-3, he never lost contact with England, and was instrumental in founding the Berlin Academy of Sciences in 1700. As a senior of the Unity of Brethren he tried to help his co-religionists in Bohemia and Hungary. He spared no pains to help the Duke of Transylvania, Francis II Rákóczi, in his struggle against the Habsburgs. Acting as an intermediary and accompanied by one of Rákóczi's agents, J. M. Klement, a native of Banská Bystrica in Slovakia, he came to England in 1709 and was even received by the Whig government under Marlborough and Godolphin. The mission, however, did not change the course of the Hungarian War, which was brought to an end in 1711 by a Habsburg victory.

Although the old Unity of Brethren was powerless, it did not cease to exist. Under the name of Moravian Brethren, its followers provided one of the stimuli for the English religious revival initiated by John Wesley (1738). The seats of the Moravians, Herrnhut in Germany, Fulneck near Leeds, Chelsea and Fetter Lane in London, remained as reminders of Hus and the Unity of Brethren until the holocaust of World War II.

The interest in the "Land of the Martyrs", however, was losing its unique appeal and the literary picture of Bohemia was again conveniently vague and mildly exotic. We should not take for granted Lady Mary Wortley Montagu's description of Prague from her first visit (1716): "The kingdom of Bohemia is the most desert of any I have seen in Germany; the villages are poor and the posthouses so miserable, clean straw and fair water are blessings not always to be found, and better accommodation not to be hoped... This town (Prague) was once the royal seat of the Bohemian kings, and is still the capital of the kingdom. There are as yet some remains of its former splendour, being one of the largest towns in Germany, but for the most part old built and thinly inhabited, which makes the houses very cheap, and those people of quality, who cannot easily bear the expense of Vienna, choose to reside here where they have assemblies, music, and all other diversions at very moderate rates, all things being here in great abundance, especially the best wild-fowl I ever tasted. I have been already visited by some of the most considerable ladies, whose relations I knew at Vienna..." Lady Mary Montagu evidently did not like Bohemia and was not much impressed by the Prague ladies either. Her *Letters*, published in 1763, probably did less harm than might be expected to English ideas on Bohemia.

The English reading public learned about Bohemia, whose name appeared in the papers from time to time during the War of the Austrian Succession (1740-8) and, later, during the Seven Years' War (1756-63), from more popular books, like *The Complete English Scholar*, published in 1753 by James Buchanan. "Which is the chief city of Bohemia?" asks Buchanan and gives the answer: "Prague... the Capital of Bohemia, situated on the River Mulde, 140 Miles N. W. of Vienna, 100 N. E. of Ratisbon, & 70 S. of Dresden. It is the largest City in Europe, & the most populous next to London, Paris & Constantinople; encompassed with a Wall, Bastions, & other Works, which render it as strong as a Place of that Extent can be: but it is commanded by several Hills. It stands pleasantly, surrounded by fine Fields and Gardens, & is adorned with a great many elegant Houses, Churches & Convents. There is scarce any City that hath more Nobility & wealthy People residing in it, & these are extremely polite and civil to Strangers. This fine City was a few Years ago plundered by the French & Prussians."

In general, English 18th-century geographies and histories, including Hume's *History of Great Britain*, knew of the existence of the Kingdom of Bohemia and its capital but they were silent regarding the Czech (still called Bohemian) people. This attitude led the British press, and later historians, to write of the battles at Kolin, Austerlitz and Königgrätz (in Czech Kolín, Slavkov and Hradec Králové). While the fate of British power was being decided on Czech territory, the use of German place names was indicative of the fact that the Czechs were of small account as a nation in the policies of the day. Up to 1918 practically all Austrian official and semi-official atlases and other geographical publications gave German names only and so English writers are hardly to blame, as they had no Czech sources at their disposal.

When Dr Burney, the father of Fanny Burney, came to Bohemia and described it in his *German Tour* (1773), he saw the poverty of the Czech peasants but noticed also their admirable musical abilities. Czech musicians were known in London. J. L. Dussek's compositions, *The Battle of Prague* (1790) and *The Sufferings of the Queen of France* (1793), brought the message of musical Bohemia, then providing a congenial background for Mozart's music.

Laurence Sterne, too, found Bohemia a good place for the location of his "Story of the King of Bohemia and His Seven Castles" told but never finished by Corporal Trim in *The Life and Opinions of Tristram Shandy* (1760), but Sterne's Irish countrymen knew better. Of the old families of adventurers turned Bohemian landowners in the 17th century, only the Leslies and Taaffes remained. Evidently the Leslies were mainly interested in a possible heritage in Scotland, but a young Count Taaffe informed his English friends about the opposition of the Bohemian nobility to Emperor Josef II and his ideals of "Enlightened Despotism". These ideals were, of course, criticized from a different viewpoint by other Irishmen, who did not come to Bohemia until the 18th century, including the MacNeven family, which became closely linked with the history of Prague University. One of its members, William James MacNeven, studied medicine in Prague and later returned to Dublin and practised there. In 1797, he joined the United Irishmen, was arrested and banished for life. He died as a champion of the Irish in America (1841). Another Irishman, Lieutenant-Colonel of the Imperial armies, Count Wallis, even learned the Czech language and was, according to his friend, the Czech patriot Jan Jeník of Bratřice, a supporter of the

Czech National Revival, which he compared to the struggle of the Irish. Another Irishman, Dr O'Reilly, was a friend of the aging Giacomo Casanova, while J. F. Opiz, a Bohemian admirer of the French revolution, entered into correspondence with that curious figure, Lord Gordon of the Gordon Riots. Both Opiz and O'Reilly were among the Bohemian "Jacobins", Opiz being a keen reader of Tom Paine's pamphlets. A fine collection of Radical tracts was in the possession of the Parishes, an interesting family of merchants and bankers, who came from Leith via Hamburg to Vienna. David Parish had a turbulent career as a banker-adventurer, for a time acted as an intermediary in financial affairs between the British and the Austrian government, brought the Rothschild family to Austria, and finally committed suicide. His brother, John Parish, settled in Žamberk in Bohemia and his descendants continued to be genuinely interested in Czech history.

Romanticism opened up new channels for cultural influences between the two countries. While translating Schiller's *Wallenstein Trilogy* from German (1799-1800), Coleridge was fascinated by the figure of Wallenstein. Another member of the Taaffe family lived in Pisa with Byron, and John Bowring, secretary of Byron's Committee for Aid to Greece, a linguist and a pupil of Jeremy Bentham, became the first modern translator from the Czech. In 1832, he published his *Cheskian Anthology* containing a survey of "poetical literature" in Bohemia. Bowring was the first to differentiate between "Bohemian" and "Czech". The same year the book arrived secretly in Prague and Jan Jeník of Bratřice, Czech writer and chronicler of the Czech National Revival, wrote in his *Diary* of the joy with which he had read Bowring's words that "Time will tear away the scrolls which falsehood has attached to the histories

WÝBOR Z BÁSNICTWI ČESKÉHO.

CHESKIAN ANTHOLOGY:

BEING

A HISTORY OF THE

Poetical Literature of Bohemia,

WITH TRANSLATED SPECIMENS

BY

JOHN BOWRING.

Prawan wlast gen w srdci nosíme,
Tuto nebze bíti ani krásti.

KOLLAR.

Our heart—our country's casket and defence—
Our country, none shall steal—none tear it thence.

Hudbu a zpěwy Čech milug.

LONDON:

ROWLAND HUNTER, St. PAUL'S CHURCH-YARD.

1832

The title page
of the first English survey
of Czech literature.

of Žižka, Hus and George of Podiebrad, and write Patriot, Reformer and Hero, and these words will be indelible..." Bowring was in contact with the younger generation of Czech writers, especially the group of Jungmann and Čelakovský, but he also had some contacts with the "Grand Old Man" of Czech literature, Josef Dobrovský.

The Czech National Revival, made possible by the fact that the Czech language and culture had not been stifled by the Habsburg policy of Germanization, was the result of the zealous efforts of countless patriots of the late 18th century. But it was also the result of the great changes in the social and economic life of the country. The early years of the 19th century saw the beginning of the Industrial Revolution in Central Europe. Large-scale industrialization brought to the fore new social classes, the proletariat and the bourgeoisie, and raised the social standing of the middle classes in the provinces. Czech peasants, Czech burghers, and sections of the Czech working classes formed a new social background for literary life.

From the very beginnings of this revival, English culture was one of the weapons the Czechs used against the hegemony of German influences. Bohemian libraries of the late 18th century were full of English books and the knowledge of English literature and philosophy was considerable from 1771 onwards, when the *Prague Learned Journal* began to be published.

When Czech books began to be issued in larger numbers, V. M. Kramerius published Defoe's *Robinson Crusoe* and Bacon's *New Atlantis*. Percy's *Reliques* led to the imitation of popular poetry, and Slovakia produced the first translations of contemporary English poetry. Hamlet's soliloquy (To be or not to be) was translated by the Slovak poet Tablic in his book *Poezye* in 1806, and in 1831 Tablic compiled the first anthology of English poetry, *Anglické*

In 1620 companies of British volunteers went to help the Czechs
in their fight against the Imperial armies.
A pamphlet by John Taylor.

AN
ENGLISH-MANS
LOVE TO Bohemia:
WITH
A friendly Farewell to all the noble Souldiers that goe
from great Britaine to that honorable Expedition.
AS ALSO,
The names of the most part of the Kings, Princes, Dukes, Mar-
quisses, Earles, Bishops, and other friendly Confederates, that
are combined with the Bohemian part.
By IOHN TAYLOR.

Printed at Do— M.DC.XX

John Amos Comenius (1592—1670), the educationist
and philosopher, lived in England as an exile
in 1641-2.
(Portrait by G. Glover.)

Hollar's view of part of Westminster
(about 1647) was used on a British
stamp commemorating the 700th anniversary
of Parliament.

Wenceslas Hollar (1607—77),
a Czech artist who spent many years in England.

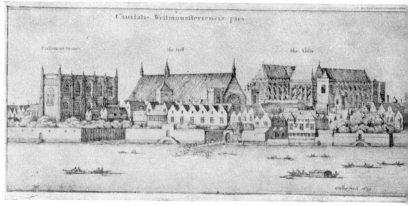

WENCESLAUS HOLLAR

View of London by Canaletto, National Gallery, Prague.

Charles I and Henrietta Maria by Van Dyck,
Kroměříž Castle Gallery.

Lady Vaux by Hans Holbein,
National Gallery, Prague.

Hluboká Castle in southern Bohemia was rebuilt
in Tudor Gothic style after 1841 by Princess Schwarzenberg.

Brno, the second largest town in Czechoslovakia, owes its economic importance to engineering and textile industries.

Antonín Dvořák (1841-1904) was awarded the honorary doctor's degree by Cambridge University in 1891.

Musy v československém oděvu (English Muses in Czechoslovak Garb). Milton's *Paradise Lost* was translated by Josef Jungmann, the master and model of Czech translators from English.

English literature reached Central Europe by many different channels. The landed aristocracy were very "Anglophile" from the days of the French Revolution. This led to the superficial imitation of some aspects of the life of the English leisured classes. English jockeys were the vogue, and Princess Schwarzenberg was so impressed by Tudor Gothic, that she had Hluboká Castle (in Southern Bohemia) reconstructed in imitation of Windsor Castle. Her brother, Prince Felix Schwarzenberg, won notoriety as a young military attaché in London thanks to his love affair with Lady Jane Ellenborough. This did not prevent him from becoming later, as Austrian Prime Minister (1848-51), a passionate adversary of Palmerston. Members of the Bohemian aristocracy, for instance the young Counts Thun, completed their education in England and had many friends among the English liberals and Catholics.

At least some of the aristocrats realised that the Industrial Revolution was bound to spread from England to the heart of Europe. The Archbishop of Olomouc, Archduke Rudolf, consciously imitated the English example when he laid the foundations of the Vítkovice Iron Works near Ostrava, and sent his chief adviser, Professor Riepl, more than once to get information in England, where he made the acquaintance of Stephenson. He brought a group of English and Welsh specialists to the Vítkovice works. Another group of South-Wales iron-workes and smelters spent several years in northern Moravia helping the Lieutenant General of Moravia, Count Mittrowsky, to start his large modern ironworks at Sobotín and Štěpánov. Mittrowsky did his best to arrange for a comfortable and pleasant stay for these welcome helpers, who requested, among other amenities, a supply of new books in English.

On the other hand, young noblemen on their "Grand Tour" of Europe were not the only Czech visitors to England. During the first half of the 19th century, Czech chemists, technicians and engineers journeyed to Great Britain in increasing numbers. In the forties some peasants from the hop-growing districts of North Bohemia, technically still burdened with labour rents though no longer (since 1781) serfs, came to Kent to see the new system of props then introduced in English hop-gardens.

A number of English specialists decided to settle in Central Europe. During the thirties, the "English" machineworks were founded at Karlín, a suburb of Prague, by a Mr Ruston, in the vicinity of works owned by Joseph Lee and Evans. The Englishman Bracegirdle established the machineworks at Brno in 1844, and the first engineering factory supplying the North Bohemian textile industry with machinery was built at Liberec. All this was only the beginning of the process of industrialization, which did not culminate until after the revolutionary period of 1848-9. The majority of Czech people still lived by farming and the course of the Industrial Revolution only partially affected their lives.

Only the most far-sighted members of the Czech intelligentsia viewed with apprehension the social changes taking place in England. Big industrial enteprises were still in foreign hands and therefore the fate of the small man was often equated with that of the Czech nation. But in general, the English parliamentary system was a model for young Czech politicians, including František Palacký, the historian. Palacký modelled his imposing *History of the Czech Nation* on the works of Hume and Robertson, which he had read during his student years at Bratislava, although in a rather haphazard way.

It is remarkable that an early description of the geography of the British Isles was published in the small Central Slovak town of Banská Bystrica. The *Geography*, compiled in 1798 by Ladislav Bartolomeides, was republished several times. In 1847 K. V. Zap, a young radical and Slavophile, published his *General Geography* with a modernized description of the United Kingdom. Czech literary magazines of the period, *Květy* (Blossoms), *Česká včela* (Czech Bee — possibly after the English model), and *Poutník* (Pilgrim), published the first translations of English short stories. M. Fialka became the first of the Czech "Dickensians" before 1848. We can say that apart from Shakespeare and Milton, Charles Dickens, Walter Scott, Lord Byron and Bulwer-Lytton were the favourite authors of the young Czech reading public before 1848. Czech papers regularly carried articles "on social life in England", written by the founders of modern Czech journalism, Karel Havlíček Borovský, K. V. Zap and Jakub Malý. While the "Pilgrim" was a wholehearted admirer of English political life, *Pražské Noviny* (Prague Journal) edited by Havlíček was much more critical. It published articles on the Chartist movement and especially on the Irish fight for Home Rule. Havlíček's purpose was very simple: he used the analogy between the struggle of the Irish against London and that of the Czechs against Vienna. Thus the "Irish Problem" became extremely popular in Bohemia, and the first radical-democratic association, of which curiously enough the formidable secret police of Metternich's régime knew nothing, received the name of *Repeal*. Knowledge of the situation in England was, necessarily, scanty. The young radical J. V. Frič, a student who broke free of his family ties and went as far as London, was deeply shocked by the fact that the good "Lord" Bowring did not show the same interest in the Czech cause in 1845 as he had displayed in his book thirteen years before.

The term "Bohemian" was at this time introduced by Thackeray, perhaps under the French influence, to designate socially unconventional persons. This added to the confusion of the English readers, for whom Thomas Carlyle re-wrote the tale of Libussa, a princess from Czech mythology, and included it in his *German Tales* (1827). The historian of Frederick the Great did not show much understanding for the Czechs and recommended some refugees to learn Russian and become Russianized as soon as possible. But books on Bohemia and the Czechs and their literature were growing in numbers and quality. B. A. Granville, John Strong and G. R. Gleig provided useful information for English readers on the complicated situation in the Austrian Empire, which had been sharply criticised by a refugee from a Prague monastery, Karl Postl, known as Charles Sealsfield.

Sympathetic observers, however, formed a tiny minority. The Czech reading public was, on the whole, better and more accurately informed than its English counterpart. Practically all the political terminology used by the Czech opposition to the Austrian government was of English origin, and England was, as Havlíček once wrote, the teacher of the Czech people in political affairs, at a time when France was the model of *haute couture* and Germany the seat of philosophy. Such was the situation in the first months of 1848 when, with the coming of the "Spring of European Peoples", the old despotic régime in Central Europe crumbled and its representative, the hated Prince Metternich, sought refuge in disguise in Brussels and Brighton.

5

The struggle of the Czechs and Slovaks for independence begins with the frustration of their hopes for justice and a peace-loving Austrian monarchy. The attempts to make Austria both democratic and federalist were defeated in the years 1848-9 when it became clear that neither the old ruling classes, intent on restoring feudal despotism, nor the rising ruling classes, the Austrian and the Hungarian bourgeoisie, were willing or able to serve the cause of nationalities. This does not mean that the policy of the Czech and Slovak leaders was irreproachable. They had no conception of organizing a nation-wide movement, did not seek to win the peasants for democracy and viewed the workers with suspicion. Unwittingly, with their obstinate faith in "Austro-Slavism" and a righteous Austrian federal monarchy, they played into the hands of a junta of military commanders and frightened landowners. The revolutionary movement was thwarted step by step by counter-revolution: in Prague by the end of June 1848, in Vienna by the end of October 1848, and in Hungary and Northern Italy in the summer of 1849.

Taking advantage of the brief period of freedom of the press, the Czech newspapers of the time followed the situation in Great Britain with interest. On this occasion the Chartists rather than the Irish attracted attention. Their defeat in April, 1848, was regarded as a severe blow to the "Revolutionary Spring".

The first steps in introducing parliamentary procedure were modelled upon the Parliament of Westminster. In an article of December, 1848, Havlíček stressed that English terminology prevailed in the dealings of the Diet, which had moved from Vienna to the quiet Moravian town of Kroměříž. And in fact, the acts of the Diet abound with terms like "budget", "bill", "amendment". When the German bourgeoisie with their "Greater German" aspirations organized a congress of their representatives at Teplice, Robert Noel, "an English-man, living near Děčín", rightly saw it as a dangerous step. But the days of congresses and parliaments were soon ended. The Diet at Kroměříž was dispersed by a military *coup d'état*, staged by Prime Minister Schwarzenberg. The draft of a new constitution was turned down because it had been put forward by revolutionaries.

When the Czech and German Radical Democrats of Bohemia made their last attempt in spring, 1849, to prevent the triumph of the counter-revolution by joining forces with the revolutionary move-ment in Saxony, their designs were thwarted and the young men who took part in this "May Sedition" were either arrested, like J. V. Frič, or had to flee. While old Prince Metternich could now leave hospitable England — Czech papers openly deplored the fact that in 1848 England had been the last refuge of dyed-in-the-wool reactionaries — his political rivals moved in. Thus the Radicals of both nationalities left Bohemia in 1849 for England; the Germans Meissner, Ebert and Hartmann, the Czechs Rieger, Straka and Springer. The most remarkable of them was, at that time, Dr A. Springer, who in 1848-9 lectured in Prague on "The History of the Age of Revolutions" (1789-1848). In his lectures, published in 1849, Springer made use of Engels's *The Condition of the Working Class in England* as source material. He was the first representative at Prague University of the modern type of philosophical historian. Despite all his dependence upon literature, his uncritical approach and inclination to anecdote and hearsay, Springer was by far the ablest historian lecturing at the University in the first half of the 19th century.

Another fruit of freedom of the press was the first Czech history of England (*Děje anglické země*, 1849), written by J. S. Tomíček and published by the Czech National Museum in the New Czech Library series. Although Tomíček's History was no original work, it nevertheless provided a good survey of English history up to 1820, and was fairly successful among the reading public eager to know more about Palmerston's England.

It is not without interest to follow the response which the revolution and counter-revolution in Bohemia and Austria aroused in the contemporary English press. On the whole one can say that the mildly liberal *Times*, the conservative *Morning Chronicle* and the liberal *Economist* were all much more sympathetic to the views of the German bourgeoisie and had little sympathy for the Slavonic movements on the Continent. On the other hand, the papers edited by the Fraternal Democrats, the *Northern Star* for example, and the Chartist papers, *The Reasoner* and the *Cause of the People*, made common cause with the Czechs.

The *Economist* carried commentaries by its Leipzig correspondent, who did not like the Czechs at all. On June 10th he wrote that the Slavs who, like all semi-civilized peoples, were disposed to violence and rage, would soon need the German intelligentsia, so that the German element would certainly be triumphant. The June street fighting in Prague, nevertheless, led him to acknowledge that the Slavs and the Czechs, of whom next to nothing had so far been heard, had now started some sort of national existence *(The Economist*, June 24th, 1848).

The *Times* sided even more openly with the German bourgeoisie, advancing the view that the German Union (probably the *Zollverein*, or the old *Bund)* should be entitled to use force to bring the rebellious Slavs to reason. The unequal struggle of students and workers against the cold-blooded repression initiated by Field-Marshal

Windischgrätz was qualified as a "war of races", "plundering by the rabble", a pernicious revolution, while the massacre provoked by Windischgrätz was hailed as an act of statesmanship. *The Times* editorial of 29th June, 1848, expressed satisfaction that the "forces of order" had suppressed the dangerous Slavonic congress and the "popular party" endangering "public order" and welcomed the reassumption of power by the "authorities". Soon afterwards, however, *The Times* ceased to favour the Austrian Government and strongly criticised its "terrorism". As a result the paper's correspondent in Vienna was subjected to the usual police chicaneries.

The reaction of the Chartists was different. Their leader, Ernest Jones, published in March 1848 a poem which stressed the revolutionary tradition of the Czech Hussites *(Northern Star*, 18th March). In April, Jones began to publish in the last issued number of the *Labourer* a series of articles on the Rising of the Working Classes with a short history of the Czech Hussite movement, written probably under the influence of the *History of the French Revolution* by Louis Blanc. Other Chartists, for example, W. L. Lington and G. J. Holyoake, were influenced by the Italian revolutionary nationalist Giuseppe Mazzini in their sympathies towards the Slavs in Austria. Mazzini, on the other hand, relied on John Bowring's older articles in his essay *On the Slavonic Movement*. Mazzini's ideas were proclaimed by the Chartist poet Thomas Cooper, in *The Slavonic People — An Oration*, in a lecture about the "Slovacs, who inhabit W. Hungary and the Slovenzi (Slovenes)" and generally about the struggles of the Slavonic nations with the Magyars, "who until lately held complete sovereignty over the Slavonic inhabitants of Hungary" *(The Reasoner*, August 13th and 20th).

A counterpart to Tomíček's book on English history and a continuation of the work started by Bowring (who died in 1872) was the achievement of a real enthusiast for Czech literature, the Reverend Albert Henry Wratislaw (died in 1859), Headmaster of Bury St. Edmund's School, whose ancestors had come to England at the end of the 18th century. We do not know much about them. Perhaps they arrived in a similar way as various other unconnected individuals who only come to our knowledge exceptionally, like that "man" of James Boswell, "Joseph Ritter, a Bohemian, a fine stately fellow above six feet high" who appears in 1773 to have attended Dr Johnson and Boswell on their *Tour to the Hebrides* (1785). Certainly, the Reverend Albert Wratislaw claimed to be a descendant of the noble family of the same name, but he was probably wrong in this.

In 1849, Wratislaw published his *Lyra Czecho-Slovanská* (Bohemian Poems Ancient and Modern), with a short introductory essay. He was probably in contact with J. Malý, then editor of *Pražský prostonárodní list* (Prager Popular Review), through which "Professor Wratislaw" had been known in Bohemia since 1851. Forty years later Wratislaw published *Sixty Folk Tales from Exclusively Slavonic Sources* (1889) based on K. J. Erben's folk tales. This literary folklore seems to have gained favour with the English reading public.

In the spring of 1850, F. L. Rieger, the future son-in-law of F. Palacký and heir to his political role, came to London in the company of Robert Noel and the historian Springer. In his letters to Havlíček he stressed the interest he took in the English press, in economic and social life. Evidently, he was most impressed by the "factory area" in the North. He was received by Palmerston and discussed the Eastern Question with him. The result of this journey was a book, published in 1860, *Industry and Its Progress in Its Relation to the Freedom and Wealth of the People*. It was meant to be his "habilitation" thesis and the beginning of his academic career, but it was never accepted. Rieger endeavoured to show that the Czech bourgeoisie had nothing to fear from the Industrial Revolution and tried, moreover, to encourage the initiative of Czech industrialists. His companion, A. Springer, was much less optimistic. In the years 1850-1 Springer published *Studie sociálního života v Anglicku* (Studies of Social Life in England) in the review of the Czech National Museum. He saw in England a model of democratic life and defended it against criticism. On the other hand, he was aware that England was a "political paradise" but a "social hell". The origins of poverty in England were caused, in his opinion, by unequal division of wealth. He thought that pauperism was a nuisance and advocated the establishment of polytechnical schools in the East End of London.

We do not know whether the third Czech refugee also came in the company of Robert Noel, the Englishman who had lived for many years in Northern Bohemia, and whom Prof. Haight, quoting from Lady Noel Byron's letters, describes as "cultivated, much-travelled, a noted phrenologist in that golden age of phrenology, and the friend of many well-known men and women". This third new-comer was by far the most romantic personality. A. V. Straka stud-ied divinity in Leipzig in 1848, took part in the radical movement and was among the organizers of the "May Sedition" of 1849. He was sentenced to death *in absentia* and could not return home. He taught for some time at the Landsdowne House Academy, in 1862 published an English Grammar in Prague and finally became Pro-fessor of German at University College, London. In the fifties,

Straka is said to have had close relations with the Russian radicals A. I. Herzen and Mikhail Bakunin.

It is also unknown whether Straka ever met George Eliot, as we know for certain that Springer and Noel did. In July 1851, George Eliot wrote about an "interesting visit" by two gentlemen. She was clearly much taken with one of them "a Dr Springer, a Bohemian patriot — a man of great talent and acquirements with the finest possible eyes — such eyes as do not grow in England". According to Ian Milner (*Herr Klesmer: George Eliot's Portrait of the Artist,* 1964) Springer, and possibly also Noel, with their radical sympathies, tempered by a post-revolutionary sobriety, appealed strongly to George Eliot and supplied the positive values with which she endowed Herr Klesmer, one of the protagonists of her *Daniel Deronda.* Klesmer, according to his rival, is "a Pole, or a Czech, or something of that fermenting sort, in a state of political refugeeism".

But George Eliot was an exception in the world of Victorian conformism, and thus the sojourn of political refugees such as Straka, Springer or a few years later J. V. Frič went for the most part unnoticed. The Bohemia that was again becoming better known was not the Bohemia of revolutionaries, but the old harmless Bohemia of good kings and queens. The fifties saw the composition of the Christmas carol about Good King Wenceslas. It was forgotten that 15th-century England had also known this saint, and the Rev. J. M. Neale, Director of Sackville College, used the version of the legend published in 1847 in Prague,

"Good King Wenceslas looked out
On the feast of Stephen",

and could thus bring the Christmas spirit to the streets of English towns and villages and even to the resolute Britons bearing the White Man's Burden in far-away India (as we see in Rudyard Kipling's story *William the Conqueror*). And so Bohemia remained "associated with wild and wonderful legends of the rude barbaric ages", without any culture and civilisation, with a "language of one of those rude Slavonian tribes whose original home was in the vast steppes of Central Asia" (Bayard Taylor). Fashionable writers, like Louise de la Ramée (Ouida) in her *Strathmore*, believed quite seriously that Gypsies in Bohemia had Slavonic features, that their language was a dialect of the Czech etc. This tradition is alive also in the novel *Nina Balatka, the Story of a Maiden of Prague* by Anthony Trollope (1867). The only antidote to this type of literature were stories, hardly less unrealistic, about the "land of Huss". Although one of the leading correspondents of *The Times*, Stephen Opper de Blowitz, was born in Bohemia, the newspaper carried news from Bohemia only very exceptionally, for instance, during the Austro-Prussian War of 1866.

Only the last three decades of the 19th century produced works which spread knowledge of the Czech language, literature and history among English-speaking people. In 1889 the first Oxford Slavist, Richard William Morfill, brought out *A Grammar of the Bohemian or Czech Language*, the first Czech text-book for Englishmen, which unfortunately did not have many successors. Professor S. R. Gardiner was the first modern English historian who, in his *England and Germany at the Beginning of the Thirty Years' War*, tackled a specifically Czech problem. Gardiner's friend, Prof. Gindely from Prague University, was probably the first Czech historian, since Comenius' *History of the Persecution of the Bohemian Church*, whose work was translated into English; incidentally, yet another book on 17th century history, *History of the Thirty Year's War* (1884). R. W. Morfill wrote a book on *Slavonic Literatures* (1883).

The old Bohemia was re-discovered by the members of a mission sent to Central Europe by the Church of Scotland. Soon afterwards novels appeared, especially in Scotland, dealing with the Czech past much more realistically than any previous works. Scottish Calvinism also influenced the work of Czech Protestant writers, among them Čeněk Dušek and Jan Karafiát, author of *Fireflies* (Broučci, 1876), at one time an immensely popular tale for children. In many cases the same people informed the Czech public about the widening vistas of English literature. Charles Dickens continued to be the most popular of English authors, and Jan Neruda and Svatopluk Čech were among his Czech admirers. *Jane Eyre*, "the orphan of Lowood", was popular from the seventies. The novels of George Eliot were much less understood. Translations of her books were published in the *Anglická knihovna* (English Library) series, which also introduced works by Oscar Wilde, George Meredith, George Moore and H. G. Wells. Before the Great War, H. G. Wells probably headed the best-seller list. Thackeray's novels were translated into Czech by the first Czech English scholar, V. E. Mourek, Professor at Prague University, author of a first, rather conservative, *Survey of the History of English Literature* (1890), and editor of the first English-Czech dictionary (1879). Professor Josef Janko popularised the works of Shakespeare *(Shakespeare, His Life and Works,* 1912). The first Professor of English language and literature, Vilém Mathesius, the real founder of English studies in Bohemia, began his *History of English Literature* in 1910 and helped to bring the works of Shakespeare to the Czech audience.

Mathesius succeeded in preparing the Shakespeare Celebration of 1916, staged in the midst of the First World War, as an act of faith in the humanist values of English culture. Making use of a tradition started as early as 1864, he managed to give the occasion great political weight. At the very beginning of the new upsurge of Czech national effort, a group of Czech artists, writers and politicians, united in the Artists' Club (Umělecká Beseda), had decided in August, 1863, to organize great celebrations in honour of the "English bard", probably as a counterpoise to the impact of German culture. After many difficulties, the Shakespeare Festival was held in the Prague Provisional Theatre on April 23rd, 1864. Among those who actively participated were young artists (Karel Purkyně) and young authors (Jan Neruda, Vítězslav Hálek, E. Züngel and others). The Czech composers Bedřich Smetana and Zdeněk Fibich also contributed. The sweet figure of Shakespeare's Perdita *(Perdita ars bohemica* — the forlorn art of Bohemia) was made a symbol of the renewal of Czech culture. Five days later, the Artists Club organized another small celebration, this time for its members only, introduced by the first Czech paper on the history of Shakespeare's dramatic art to be read in Bohemia. The celebrations resulted in a decision to complete the publication of Shakespeare's works in Czech translation. *The Dramatic Works of William Shakespeare* were published by the Matice Česká in the years 1855-1872. It is remarkable that Neruda, one of the participants in the 1864 celebrations, wrote in his essay, *Modern Man and the Arts*, that apart from Shakespeare, socialist art should appear on the Czech stage (1867).

Only through music could 19th-century Czech culture repay its debt to England. From the eighties Antonín Dvořák's music made its impact on English culture, as his works were introduced to the public thanks to Novello, Ewes and Co. and his English friends. The first performance of the oratorio *St. Ludmila* took place in Leeds in 1886, with an English text by Rev. Troutbeck and notes by J. Bennett. *The Spectre's Bride* was performed one year earlier in Birmingham. Dvořák's compositions have ever since featured in the repertoires of British orchestras, and his music became the symbol of a new era in Anglo-Czech cultural relations. Here was one field where progress could be made without misunderstanding caused by the medium of communication.

Apart from Mourek and Janko, other professors of the Prague

Bratislava, the Slovak capital on the Danube. From an old print.

Czech University helped to foster understanding between the two nations. T. G. Masaryk introduced to the Czech public some English philosophers of the 19th century, including John Stuart Mill and Thomas Carlyle, and gave his review the name of *Athenaeum*. In the London review of the same name, between 1891 and 1904, Václav Tille published reports on the state of Czech literature. In 1896 Fisher and Unwin published Charles Edmund Maurice's *Bohemia: from the earliest times to the fall of national independence in 1620.*

In the same year, Francis Lützow, scion of an old noble family which had its estates in Eastern Bohemia, published a booklet entitled *Bohemia, An Historical Sketch*. Lützow was the secretary of the Austrian embassy in London until 1890, and a member of the Austrian Diet for four years. His book was not very original but its style was lively. His stress on the glorious past of Hussite Bohemia could not fail to bring him success among British, and especially Protestant readers. Lützow was a member of the parliamentary opposition and sharply criticised the Vienna government in an article on *The Bohemian Question*, which appeared in *The Nineteenth Century* (1898). In 1899 he published his *History of Bohemian Literature*, translated Comenius' *Labyrinth of the World* into English and in 1902 thousands of delighted readers welcomed his book, *The Story of Prague*, published in the "Medieval Towns" series. In 1904 he was invited to Oxford to deliver the Ilchester Lectures on the historians of Bohemia (published as *Lectures on the Historians of Bohemia*, 1905). A year later he brought out his second important work, *The Life and Times of John Hus*, based on works by Czech historians, beginning with František Palacký.

At a time when the Czech bourgeois politicians were tentatively trying to make direct international contacts, Lützow's aid proved invaluable. He helped to organize the Czech section of the 1906 Austrian exhibition in London, was a member of the first Czech Olympic Games Committee, and helped the City of Prague to set up its first information centre. Slowly, this old-fashioned "Bohemian" patriot was becoming an ardent Czech nationalist. He enlightened the Czech reading public on new trends in English literature, defended Czech historiography against German attacks, and supplied the *Encyclopaedia Britannica* with readable articles on Bohemia and the Hussites.

The prospects of federalism, which he considered the only possible salvation for Austria, were not too hopeful in the decade preceding 1914. Lützow saw dark clouds gathering on the horizon. In the approaching conflict between the Czechs and Vienna he had taken sides long before Sarajevo. He was much more realistic than those prominent Czech historians who did not see the importance of the struggle for universal suffrage and were evidently still impressed by the Habsburgs. His growing radicalism can be traced in an article on *The Position of the Bohemian Nation in Austria* (1906), a study *Later Thoughts on the Apostles of Moravia and Bohemia* (1911) and his last work on *The Hussite Wars* (1914).

It is, therefore, not difficult to understand Lützow's attitude towards Austria-Hungary after 1914. He was the only member of the Bohemian aristocracy openly to oppose Vienna. The Czech edition of his *Bohemia* (published in 1911) was one of the first books to be confiscated. In 1915, when T. G. Masaryk began his struggle against the Habsburgs with a lecture on Hus in Geneva, and when R. W. Seton-Watson gave a similar lecture at King's College, London, Lützow wrote two papers, *The Martyrdom of John Hus* and a *Message to the Preachers of To-day*. On 13th January 1916, still unrepentant, he died in exile in Switzerland. He was a well-informed writer, sincerely interested in the history of the Czech nation, of which he became a member of his own choice. His books were well written and usually gave an adequate picture of historical events, as they were then understood. There is no better compliment for a historian than the fact that his books are still read nearly three quarters of a century after they were written.

It is true, of course, that most of Lützow's friends belonged to the older generation and that he was probably much more active in the English milieu than in Bohemia. The interest in all things English was still confined to the Czech upper-middle class. Immigrants to England from the Czech lands were scanty before 1914. Apart from some of the radical intellectuals (Straka was joined for several years by J. F. Frič), very few Czechs sought a new home in Britain. Probably one of the most interesting was the painter Bohuslav Kroupa, who was employed by the Canadian Pacific in the seventies and lived for several years in Canada, the United States and Central America, before becoming Professor at the Schools of Art of Edinburgh and Birmingham. In 1890, he published in London his book *An Artist's Tour (Gleanings and Impressions of Travels in North end Central America and the Sandwich Islands)* with many illustrations now of documentary value. Kroupa was heir to the traditions of the revolutionary year 1848 and a man of progressive opinions.

In 1876 the Czech working-class immigrants in London joined their Polish and Russian comrades in an eloquent plea for freedom of the Slavonic nations and for social justice. But we do not hear much about their organisation. When Eduard Beneš, then a young student of sociology, published in the Prague socialist paper *Právo lidu* (The Right of the People) a series of articles called *London and the Social Conditions in England* (September to December 1906), he did not know of any Czech working men in England. His report was glum and the author knew it: "Above all I wanted to show where a highly-developed capitalist system led, and that even in a country, where some care is taken of the worker, the reason is neither humanity nor feeling for justice, but only the egoistical endeavour to preserve a healthy labour force... It is difficult to write about the good things. There are so many bad things here, that even the good ones have a bitter taste..." For the young socialist Beneš, England was hardly an ideal: "(The English public) does not want to accept the socialist solution of this difficult problem which is the only possibility under the present circumstances. And this will make the conflict between the liberals and the working-class even sharper... On the whole it seems to me that conditions in England are a bit more squalid and worse than those in France, Germany and in our country."

When war broke out, there were about 700 Czechs and Slovaks in the United Kingdom. About 380 of them volunteered to fight against Austria-Hungary and Germany. Their organizers were F. Kopecký, a painter of miniatures, and a friend of Masaryk, and J. Sýkora, executed by the Germans in 1941. Two young British publicists shared their adverse sentiments towards the old Habsburg monarchy. They were Henry Wickham Steed, who published his highly critical book *The Habsburg Monarchy* in 1913, and R. W. Seton-Watson, alias Scotus Viator, a specialist in the nationalities problem in Austria-Hungary (*The Future of Austria-Hungary and the Attitude of the Great Powers*, 1907; *German, Slav and Magyar*, 1916).

In his book *Masaryk in England* (1943), the late Professor Seton-Watson published documents on Masaryk's stay in England in 1915-7, including his Confidential Memoranda of April 1915 and January 1916 and his famous Inaugural Lecture, given at the founding of the School of Slavonic Studies at King's College, London, October 1915, *The Problem of Small Nations in the European Crisis*. Both Seton-Watson and V. Nosek, Masaryk's collaborator, hinted at the difficulties he was to meet. The Oxford historian A. J. P. Taylor considered that Masaryk's work had gradually brought leading British politicians to agree that the Austro-Hungarian monarchy should cease to exist and that the Slav nations should regain their independence.

A. J. P. Taylor's presupposition, namely that before World War I Czechs and Slovaks were unknown in England, and that one man's work brought about the change, does not seem altogether convincing. Recent works by British historians, pupils of Seton-Watson's successor, the late Professor R. R. Betts, suggest that before 1917 Great Britain had no clear-cut policy as far as the fate of Austria-Hungary was concerned, and consequently her attitude towards the establishment of an independent Czechoslovak state was dictated by the *faits accomplis*, that is, by the break-up of the multi-national Austro-Hungarian Empire, and the revolutionary wave on the Continent. There is no doubt, however, that the independence won in 1918 marked a turning point in relations between Great Britain and the Czechoslovak Republic, a turning point prepared by long study and natural affinities no less than by the political exigencies of the moment.

6

A Czech journalist, G. Winter, writing in exile during World War II, gave the following summary of the inter-war period: "After the War, over twenty years there were fruitful contacts between Czechoslovakia and Great Britain in all fields. Czechoslovakia collaborated with Britain in the League of Nations, Czech writers, especially Čapek, were becoming popular in England and found exceptional understanding there. On the other hand, English literature never had so many enthusiastic readers as in Czechoslovakia during this period. It became clear that wherever the Czech national spirit can express itself freely, it does not fail to find response. That was seen in the success Czech music achieved in the United Kingdom. As early as the eighties Dvořák was highly successful, Czech musicians — Kubelík, the Czech Quartet — always had their British admirers, among Ševčík's pupils there were always some Englishmen and after the War Leoš Janáček had perhaps nowhere so many grateful audiences as among the British public. There were also lively economic exchanges. In 1937 Czechoslovakia exported to Great Britain and the Dominions goods amounting to 1,711 millions of Czechoslovak crowns and imported goods and raw materials to the same value. The English saw in Czechoslovakia a reliable trade partner with a sound economy and until the Munich crisis the Czechoslovak state loans were among the best papers to be had on the London Exchange." (*About England and the English*, London.)

According to A. J. P. Taylor, the wider British public distrusted the new national states that originated in 1918. The Conservatives had most of their friends among the German-speaking industrialists and landowning social strata. Labour circles considered these states a permanent danger to peace because of their national character, disregarding the core of pseudo-democratic German-speaking propaganda which was striving for a renewed German imperialism. And although a School of Slavonic Studies existed within the University of London, with Czechoslovak lecturers (Professors František Chudoba, Otakar Vočadlo, Otakar Odložilík) on its staff, and although the Prague government published *The Central European Observer* (edited by A. Brož), British government circles still had advisers who gained their knowledge of the Czechs and Slovaks from German sources.

During this whole period there were increasing opportunities for direct contacts between the British and the Czechoslovaks. Paul Selver spent many years translating from Czech and Slovak. As early as 1912, he published *An Anthology of Modern Bohemian Poetry* and became the most assiduous propagator of Czech and Slovak literature in Britain. Most of the major translations published in his *Anthology of Czechoslovak Literature* (1929) were his work, and good work, too. Selver included truly representative specimens of Czech poetry and prose, Karel Čapek, František Langer and others. He deserves special credit for acquainting the English reader with poems of such modern poets as Petr Bezruč, Jiří Wolker, S. K. Neumann, Fráňa Šrámek and others. Moreover he included well chosen specimens of Slovak literature, perhaps the first effort of this kind. In 1930 Selver published his version of the complete *Good Soldier Schweik*. The first appearance of Jaroslav Hašek's classical satire did not seem to promise any great success. But the *Good Soldier* overnight became a best-seller when it was published in an abridged form in Penguin Books in 1939.

The translations of lyrical poems by František Halas, Otakar Březina and others, the work of E. and W. Muir, did not become more widely known until the forties. The same happened with the work of two Prague writers in German, Rilke and Kafka, also translated by the pioneering Muirs.

There is no doubt that the works of Karel Čapek, fiction, prose and drama, have had the greatest success of any Czech writer among English readers. Almost all Čapek's works have been translated and published in England since 1923. The London firm of Allen and Unwin acquired most of the copyrights and as long as this publishing house was primarily interested in fiction, Čapek's works appeared on the book market at regular intervals. One of Čapek's plays, *R.U.R.*, published by the Oxford University Press in 1923, enriched the English language with the word "robot". Čapek's *Letters from England*, amused thousands of readers in the British Isles.

Many more Czech works had come out in English between the two wars. Tales, folk stories and legends, strangely enough, were among the favourites, but Czech poetry also attracted the attention of translators, especially in the twenties. The thirties seem rather meagre in comparison. Several publications of a clearly propaganda character seem to have met with little response.

The character of this publicist production can be exemplified by the following extract from one of Čapek's short articles of 1935, introducing Czechoslovakia to English readers: "A description of Czechoslovakia is impossible without indulging in a series of contradictions... it is a country old and yet new, great yet small, highly cultivated and yet very simple. It is a miscellany of so many things as to seem a vast paradox at first sight. It is beautiful, but there are possibly places more so; it is rich, but there are wealthier lands; it has a high level of culture, but there are States with a higher. Still there is perhaps no country in the world which displays such vital determination and capacity as this small nation that has held its own in Central Europe in the past and will hold its own in the future."

Three years later this capacity was put to a terrible test. In the growing international tension Czechoslovakia became the target of the expansionist attacks of Nazi Germany. The old friends of Czechoslovakia, the Wickham Steeds and the Seton-Watsons with their Liberal tradition, were out of favour with the National and Conservative Governments. That does not mean, that Czechoslovakia had few friends among the common people of Britain. But the working class was divided and even the Labour Party leaders did not see the dangers ahead, while pacifist ideas were fairly widespread. After all, what chances had young Welsh teachers and Scottish miners, Hampshire farmers and East End dockers to bring pressure to bear on a government which was steadily moving towards appeasement on the Continent — and into a political decline without precedent in British history?

A group of British students visited Czechoslovakia in April, 1938. They were a mixed batch of all possible affiliations led by Emlyn H. Garner Evans, Robert Auty and Michael Young. After their return they published a pamphlet under the title *We Saw Czechoslovakia* (London 1938). These young people were no unthinking enthusiasts and they were aware of the danger of German imperialism: "What is most refreshing to an Englishman in Czechoslovakia is that he cannot fail to identify it with Western Democracy... But what of the defence and preservation of Czech independence? The omission of Czechoslovakia from Herr Hitler's list of Germany's friends on January 30th was, to say the least, disconcerting... And yet, in face of this menace, they (the Czechs) display a fortitude hardly distinguishable from optimism... But do these pacts of mutual assistance (with France and Russia) form a certain and sufficient deterrent against an attack upon her independence? What of the guarantee of her territorial integrity under the Covenant of the League? If the failure of the League to check aggression in Manchuria spelt the defeat of the Disarmament Conference and if the overthrow of Abyssinia was the signal for a mad riotous rearmament, then any further delay on the part of the League Powers to provide security by the organisation of their common defence might well result in the downfall of civilisation. Is Czechoslovakia worth defending? To those of us who saw something of its achievements in the past eighteen years and felt something of the passion of its people for democracy and social justice, only one answer is possible. We say 'Yes'."

At about the same time, the editor of the *Survey of International Affairs, 1937,* the historian and director of the Royal Institute of International Affairs, Arnold J. Toynbee, also spoke of the League of Nations, although in a different vein: "The year 1937 saw the final eclipse of the League of Nations as an active influence on Power politics". To him the League of Nations was: "A hypocritical device for giving a moral sanction to a momentary distribution of this world's goods which was grossly inequitable", so that now new forces appear: "those of the totalitarian states to deliver the world from the disorders of communism, to secure peace with justice".

Coming from an extensive tour of Central Europe, Prof. Toynbee published a remarkable article, bearing the title *Czechoslovakia's German Problem (The Economist,* July 10, 1937). In his opinion Great Britain could not refuse to concern herself with the Central European problem. "The first reason is that our aloofness is a guarantee of our impartiality..., a second reason touches our own vital

interests. If we close our eyes to the problem of Central Europe...
we shall find ourselves in a horrible dilemma. We shall either have
to stand aside and let Germany create for herself a position in Central
Europe which will ultimately give her the whip-hand over ourselves, or else we shall have to go to war with Germany to save the
balance of power.

"Great Britain's duty and interest are to work with all her might
with those — whether in Central Europe or not — who are striving
to obtain a peaceful and a moderate solution of the Central European problem. Now is the time to act. Today the Central European
auspices are more favourable than for years past. To-morrow it may
be too late".

The article quoted was used by the gentlemen-farmers of the so-cal-
led Grusbach Circle, when during the war-years they wanted to dem-
onstrate how much they had contributed to the triumph of National
Socialism in Central Europe. Members of this group, the offspring
of the "aristocratic" families of Rohan, Khuen-Lützow, Bucquoy,
Kinsky, Clary-Aldringen, Hohenlohe-Langenburg had such good
connections that they were virtually in charge of Lord Runciman's
mission in August-September 1938. They acted as diplomatic agents
of the Henlein movement; and later as agents for Nazi circles in
Berlin. One of them, Count Dubsky, prepared unofficial contacts
between London and Berlin in January, 1938, during his journey to
London, where he was in touch with members of the "Cliveden Set".

Who were the friends of Nazi Germany, who gathered in the thirties
at the Buckinghamshire mansion of the Astor family? Michael
Astor, for a time a Conservative M. P., gives a creditable picture
of the Set in *Tribal Feeling* (1963). He claims that the members
of the Set merely supported the policy of the Chamberlain Govern-

ment: that they were politicians who used legitimate methods to propagate their views. They consisted of highly placed individuals — at least thirty peers and as many Tory M. P.s were members of the Anglo-German Fellowship or The Link — who had direct contacts with the Chamberlain-Halifax-Butler Government. The Cliveden Set had means of influence not available to those who thought that appeasing Hitler was a national disaster. According to Astor "their views were usually relayed confidentially, but frankly, to different members of the Cabinet".

Astor professes astonishment that people "almost professionally high-minded... could seriously believe that it was possible to come to any honourable arrangements with Hitler." He adds:

"In the 1930's the majority of Conservatives thought fascism was, in some ill-defined way, more or less right."

A contemporary Oxford historian, A. L. Rowse, has more to say about these "ill-defined" reasons. "They would not listen to warnings, because they did not wish to hear... they were anti-Red and that hamstrung them in dealing with the greater immediate danger to their country, Hitler's Germany" (*Appeasement: A Study in Political Decline, 1933-9*, New York, 1963). Speaking not of the Cliveden frolics, but of the discussions that were taking place at All Souls' College, Oxford, he adds: "The total upshot of their efforts was to aid Nazi Germany to achieve a position of brutal ascendancy, a threat to everybody else's security or even existence, which only a war could end."

Such were the people who "saved the peace" at Munich, "in the event bringing down the British Empire with it, too, for which they cared infinitely more than ever they did for Europe or Europe's place in the world".

The tragedy of Europe gave new impetus to the desire of British people to know more of Czechoslovakia. Some of them, for example the poet John Buckland, thought in *The Crisis, September 1938*, with a mixture of relief and shame: "Who paid the price... With heads bowed low let's realize — it was Czecho-Slovakia." Others were simply furious. "In the destruction of Czechoslovakia the entire balance of Europe was changed. Many people at the time of the September crisis thought they were only giving away the interests of Czechoslovakia, but with every month that passes you will see that they were also giving away the interests of Britain, and the interests of peace and justice" (Sir Winston Churchill, 14th March 1939).

The tragedy of Munich caused a wave of emigration. In the course of World War II many Czechs and Slovaks landed on British shores to find temporary homes. As there were quite a number of literary men and writers among them, they began to use their contacts to propagate Czechoslovak literature in Britain. Many were progressively-minded men and women who had set themselves the task of spreading knowledge of those Czech and Slovak writers who stood in the forefront of the Resistance movement in their own country. So the note of Resistance, hope, progress and socialism in many ways became the factor determining what was to be made known to British readers from Czech and Slovak literature.

Apart from Karel Čapek, who died in 1938 and whose works continued to be by far the most popular of all Czech authors, there appeared the names of Vítězslav Nezval, František Halas, Vladislav Vančura and others. Their poems were published in John Lehman's *New Writing and Daylight* or in *Review 43* or later *Review 45*. The translations of stories by Vančura were published when it was already known that the author had died a national martyr's death at the hands of the Nazis. These efforts later led to the publication of a number of anthologies of Czech poetry and prose in English translation. The list of wartime publications would be too long. But novels by British authors, Storm Jameson, Edith Pargeter, J. B. Priestley, and poems by Lewis MacNeice were further signs that the fabulous old Bohemia was dying out. Some information about Czechoslovakia even penetrated into the jealously guarded precincts of school textbooks. The numerous volumes of political literature in the years 1938-45, of short-lived importance, are too numerous to mention.

Until 1940 the Sudeten German landowners kept up contacts with their British friends, so that Prince Hohenlohe-Langenburg could visit England just before the fall of France. But then the German-English Society became useless and was quietly discarded. Berlin found better spokesmen for its aims in some Sudeten German or Austrian historians, then proudly proclaiming in the halls of the old Caroline University, from which Czech students had been sent to Sachsenhausen concentration camp, the principles of the "New European Order". Herr Heinz Zatschek, then "Commissary for the closed Czech universities", and after the war Professor at Vienna University, condemned all direct contacts the Czechs had had with England in the past and proclaimed proudly that this must never, never happen again (*England und das Reich*, Brno, 1942). His arrogant lines were written when students at Sachsenhausen concentration camp, deprived of books, living in misery and struggling for survival, were committing to memory Rudyard Kipling's *If*. At about the same time Hugh Hamilton McGoverne started under similar conditions his rendering into English of the romantic poem

May, by K. H. Mácha. His translation was published by the Prague publishing house Orbis in 1948 and was given a very favourable review in *The Times Literary Supplement*.

In the meantime, a Czechoslovak Government under President Beneš had been set up in Britain and officially recognized as an ally. Czechoslovak airmen added their quota to the achievements of the R. A. F. — and to its death-roll. The Czechs were no longer "a people of whom we know nothing", although some English landladies still expressed surprise that their tenants from Czechoslovakia were not "of the dark type". The rank-and-file Czech soldiers, airmen and workers were usually the finest representatives of their country. For the first time in history it was possible for ordinary Czechoslovaks and Britons to meet and really get to know each other.

British students, along with Czechoslovak refugee students, founded the tradition of international student cooperation, initiated after the news of the brutal suppression in Prague of student demonstrations by the Nazis on November 17th, 1939. This tradition led, after the war, to the founding of the International Union of Students. Similarly, whole sections of the British people were deeply moved by the destruction of Lidice in June 1942, and the Lidice Shall Live Committee, founded under the chairmanship of the late Dr Barnett Stross, M. P., has done much to strengthen the common struggle against Fascism. The British-Czechoslovak Friendship League has also well deserved the sympathy of the Czech and Slovak peoples.

Most of these personal links between the peoples of Czechoslovakia and Great Britain survived World War II, and even the sad years of the "Cold War". The interest in Czech and Slovak literature continued for a few years after the war, so that even some modern Czech novels (by Eduard Bass, Jiří Mucha and others) were published.

The indefatigable Paul Selver published his anthology *A Century of Czech and Slovak Poetry* with a detailed introduction under very unfavourable conditions in 1947. Undeservedly, this book is less known to the reading public than the author's other books on Czechoslovakia, e.g. his biography of T. G. Masaryk (published in 1940). Old friends re-visited Czechoslovakia; the result of a visit of a group of young politicians, led by Michael Young and Sheila Grant Duff was published late in 1946 (*Czechoslovakia: Six Studies in Reconstruction*, London, 1946). Miss Grant Duff was a member of the small circle of Socialists who saw the dangers gathering in the post-war years and threatening to destroy all possibilities of contacts between the two countries. Professor R. R. Betts belonged to the minority of British scholars who protested in vain against the severing, in the spring of 1948, of the links that had united Czech and British universities, and fought to the very end to see the cultural ties, so dear to him, renewed.

Contacts of a different type were however being established. The first Czechoslovak ice-hockey team to come over played at the Wembley Empire Pool in April 1946, and in the thick of the "Cold War" Czech athletes, with Emil Zátopek outstanding among them, competed at the London Olympic Games (1948).

A lively economic exchange has never ceased to exist either, although it continues under changed conditions, since raw materials are no longer on the list of exported and imported items. But British industrialists have become accustomed to visiting the autumn Brno Trade Fair, while Czechoslovak technicians have been following with the greatest interest the rapid progress of technology achieved in Britain in the post-war decades. These possibilities of cooperation in the economic field are far from being exhausted. Similarly, the exchange of British and Czechoslovak films has been growing. Books, paintings and old-established articles of trade such as Bohemian Glass and china have met with appreciation among those of the public who have had the opportunity of seeing the Czechoslovak Exhibitions arranged in London and elsewhere. Czechoslovak experimental dramatic companies, such as the Prague *Laterna Magika*, have also been greeted with interest, while the already traditional success attended the Czechoslovak performances during the 1964 Edinburgh Festival. The following year the Czechoslovak Film Week (staged at London's National Film Theatre) was a resounding success.

After a few years of stagnation Czechoslovak efforts to acquiant the English-speaking world with the works we consider representative of our cultural heritage began to bear some fruit. Thus, Julius Fučík's *Report from the Gallows* was published in Stephen Jolly's translation in 1951. Fore Publications brought out Vítězslav Nezval's *Song of Peace*, followed by Artia (Prague) publications of English translations of novels by Marie Majerová, Ivan Olbracht and Antonín Zápotocký. A good selection was the *Four Czech Short Stories* (by Jan Drda, Jiří Marek, Ludvík Aškenazy and Jan Weiss) published by Orbis, Prague, in 1957, and followed in 1965 by *Seven Short Stories* by young Czechoslovak writers.

The most recent period in the history of British-Czechoslovak cultural relations began in 1957. This year saw a certain revival of interest in Czech literature among the British public. The firm of Heinemann and MacMillan published some translations from the Czech by the translator-novelist Edith Pargeter. Czech readers, on their part, avidly seized upon the works of the rebellious young generation of English novelists. The homeland of Sherlock Holmes and Dr Watson has supplied the Czech public with new reading matter in the field of crime fiction, and the interest in Osborne is only one example of contemporary Czech interest in British drama. In the last decade, the British historians R. R. Betts, G. H. Holmes, W. V. Wallace, Andrew Rothstein, H. Montgomery Hyde and others have done research work in Czech archives and libraries, while monographs by B. A. Bradley, S. Zeman and others met with a good reception among Czech historians. In 1956, the quincentenary of the death of Peter Payne-Engliš, Master of Arts of the Universities of Oxford and Prague, was observed in the Senate House (Carolinum) of the Caroline University, and an address was delivered by the late Prof. R. R. Betts of the University of London. In 1957, J. D. Bernal read a paper on Comenius and the founding of the Royal Society in the course of an international conference on Comenius and his work. Prof. G. H. Turnbull and Prof. L. W. Forster also took part in the conference. Andrew Rothstein participated in a conference on the Munich crisis, organised in September 1958.

One of the high points in cultural relations was the Shakespeare celebration of 1964. Czechoslovak specialists discussed problems of Shakespeare's plays and their contemporary function at two conferences, in which, among others, Peter Brook and the Polish literary historian Jan Kott took part. Remarkable productions of *Hamlet* and *Romeo and Juliet* have achieved international success. The co-operation of Czech literary historians with L. G. Salinger and Arnold Kettle resulted in new essays written by Zdeněk Stříbrný, Zdeněk Vančura and others (and published in 1964).

Recent years have seen a rapid development of economic and cultural contacts. In 1965 exhibitions were held of the Design Centre's work in Prague and of historical Bohemian glass at the Victoria and Albert Museum in London. The Czech Philharmonic and some other musical ensembles visited England in 1965 and 1966. Dr. John Clapham concluded his long-awaited scholarly and authoritative book on *Antonín Dvořák: Musician and Craftsman* (London, Faber and Faber, 1966). In 1966 the British-inspired "Incomex 66" display of computers in Prague, the visit of the National Theatre company to London and the tour of the Royal Ballet of Czechoslovakia were further examples of cultural exchanges. In the summer of the same year the British Council and the Prague National Gallery gave the Czech and Slovak public their first opportunity to appreciate the work of Henry Moore, one of the greatest living sculptors, and in January the following year (1967) the BBC Symphony Orchestra, conducted by Sir John Barbirolli, gave a series of concerts in Czechoslovakia.

We began our account of the cultural links, connecting the home of Shakespeare's sweet Perdita with the country of its creator, so to speak, under the aegis of William Shakespeare. Young Czech literature, art and music invoked his spirit in the year 1864. It is in the spirit of Shakespeare and not in "the spirit of Munich" that we wish to conclude it. This is, of course, only a sketchy account. Most of the economic connections have been omitted, while political connections have been discussed when other than purely historical considerations have made it advisable. If we look at the tradition of purely literary connections from a quantitative point of view, we must conclude that the Czechs have so far received more than they have given. But if we look, for example, at the tradition of translations of Czech and Slovak literary works into English and compare it with the English translations of other Slavonic literature, excluding Russian of course, we can say that we do not hold the last place. The English-speaking reader seems to appreciate some of the Czech and Slovak contributions to the culture of mankind — and that is an encouraging factor which bids us continue along the lines of the past.

In 1936 John Gunther wrote in his book *Inside Europe:* "Happy is the country which has no history; there is nothing to write about Czechoslovakia". Within two years every correspondent, including Gunther, was writing about Czechoslovakia. In the world of today there is still much to be written about Czechoslovakia and her place in world affairs. It is improbable that there will be a lack of interest in Central Europe in the years to come. The relations between the peoples of present-day Czechoslovakia and Great Britain go back at least a thousand years in history. Not all of the chapters of this history are cheerful — and much of this past has often been misinterpreted and misused. But a true understanding of the past, its events, causes and consequences is, we believe, essential in a world which is endeavouring to find a peaceful solution to its problems. Let us hope that this booklet will contribute in a modest way to this understanding.

Books for Further Reading

For further information the English reader will find the following books very useful.

A good survey of Czechoslovakia's historical development is provided by František Kavka's *An Outline of Czechoslovak History*, Orbis, Prague, 1960. Back in 1945 Orbis published the first draft of the present author's essay *(England and Czechoslovakia)*, augmented in his book *Anglie a Bílá hora* (The Bohemian War and British Foreign Policy, 1618-20), Faculty of Philosophy of the Caroline University, Prague, 1949.

Information on the history of British-Czechoslovak contacts is contained in the following older publications: *Bohemian (Čech) Bibliography* by Thomas Čapek and Anna V. Čapek (Fleming H. Revell Co., New York-London 1918); *Czechoslovakia and Great Britain* by Josef A. Brož (London "Sokol", 1934); *Bohemia in Early English Literature* by René Wellek (The Slavonic and East European Review, Vol. XXI, 1943, reprinted in; René Wellek, *Essays on Czech Literature*, The Hague, Mouton & Co., 1963, pp. 81—147). Still valuable is the essay *Wyclif and Bohemia* by O. Odložilík (Prague, 1937). A Symposium on the life and work of the English Hussite Peter Payne *(Universitas Carolina*, Historica I, Prague 1957) with essays by R. R. Betts and others contains the first survey of this rich field of investigation. The last volume of *Philologica Pragensia* (published by the Czechoslovak Academy of Sciences, Prague 1964, Vol. 7/46) with articles by J. Hornát *(An Old Bohemian Legend in Elizabethan Literature)*, Ian Milner *(Herr Klesmer: George Eliot's Portrait of the Artist)*, and the Shakespeare essays by Z. Stříbrný and J. V. Polišenský are examples of the interest which English scholars in Czechoslovakia have always devoted to British-Czechoslovak literary contacts.

These contacts have also been illustrated by British authors. Thus E. J. Hobsbawm has shown in *The Age of Revolution, Europe, 1789-1848* an understanding for the problems of a crucial period of modern Czech history (London, Weidenfeld & Nicolson 1962), while Pamela R. Barnett *(Theodore Haak, F.R.S.*, The Hague, Mouton & Co., 1962) and Christopher Hill *(Intellectual Origins of the English Revolution)*, Oxford, Clarendon Press, 1965) put Anglo-Czech contacts and the work of J. A. Comenius in a completely new light.

F. G. Heymann and O. Odložilík have recently published full-length

September 1938 — a popular demonstration in London's Trafalgar Square in support of Czechoslovakia against nazi aggression.

Lord Runciman with Dr Eduard Beneš,
the President of Czechoslovakia, in August 1938,
shortly before the break-up of the Republic.

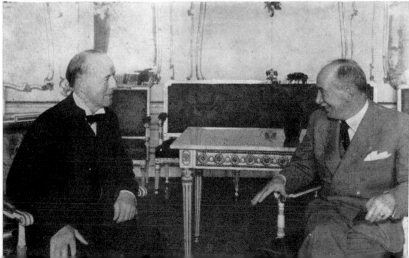

Czechoslovak airmen distinguished themselves
in the Battle of Britain.

Czechoslovak troops at Tobruk.

Inaugural meeting of the Lidice Shall Live campaign
in Stoke-on-Trent (July, 1942),
pledged to rebuild a free Lidice.

Honouring the memory of British soldiers who gave
their lives on Czechoslovak territory.
Olšany Cemetery, Prague, May 5th, 1965.

In March, 1966, the National Theatre (Prague)
gave several performances at the Aldwych Theatre.
Princess Margaret in conversation with Dr. Z. Trhlík,
Czechoslovak Ambassador.

The Royal Shakespeare Company played King Lear
at Prague's National Theatre in February, 1964.
Radovan Lukavský, a leading Czech actor,
presents Paul Scofield with a souvenir of the visit.

In November, 1966, at Wembley Stadium, Czechoslovakia held England to a goalles draw.

Part of the exhibition of Henry Moore's sculpture held
in May, 1966, in the garden adjoining the National Gallery, Prague.

Mr. Michael Stewart met Jozef Lenárt, Czechoslovak Prime Minister,
during his visit to Prague in April, 1965.

Prague with the Castle, the residence
of the President of the Czechoslovak Socialist Republic.

biographies of King George of Poděbrady, thus continuing the studies of Francis Lützow. John Clapham in *Antonín Dvořák: Musician and Craftsman* (London, Faber and Faber, 1966) gave to the English reading public an excellently written analysis of Dvořák's art of composition.

Great Britain and Czechoslovakia

Celtic Britain	*Celtic* Boii give name to Bohemia
Roman occupation of Britain	Roman "limes" along the Danube
	100
	Arrival of the *Germanic* tribes in Central Europe
410	
Germanic invasions start	
Anglo-Saxon Britain	
597	
Augustine introduces Christianity to Anglo-Saxons	**500—600**
	Slavonic tribes appear in Central Europe
	630
	Samo creates the first Slavonic realm in Central Europe
Danish invasions	*Avar invasions*
	c. 800
871	Rise of the Great Moravian Empire
Alfred the Great	
	c. 900
	Great Moravia overthrown by Magyars — Rise of Bohemia
	c. 929
	Death of "Good King Wenceslas"
	c. 1000
	Emma Regina in Bohemia
1066	
Norman Conquest	
Domesday Book	
	1085
	Vratislav I, first King of Bohemia
1154	
Henry II of Plantagenet	

1158
Vladislav, second King of Bohemia

1170
Death of Thomas Becket

1197
King Přemysl I and his adviser Robert, Bishop of Moravia

1212
The Golden Bull of Sicily

1215
Magna Charta
Richard of Cornwall elected King of Germany

1278
Richard's ally, King Přemysl II dies at Marchfeld

Hundred Years' War

1306
John of Luxemburg, King of Bohemia

1346
Black Prince wins the battle of Crécy

1346
Death of King John at Crécy

1381
Peasants' Revolt in England
Wyclif in the University of Oxford

1382
Princess Anne of Bohemia becomes Queen of England
John Hus in the University of Prague

1415
Henry V crushes the Lollards
Henry of Beaufort in Bohemia

The Wars of the Barons

1485
Tudor monarchy established

1529
Henry VIII and the English
Reformation

1554
Book of Martyrs published

1588
Triumph of Elizabethan England

1613
Princess Elizabeth marries Frederick of the Palatinate

1618
Death of Walter Raleigh

1415
The burning of John Hus

1419
The Hussite Revolution
Peter Payne active in Bohemia

1465
King of Bohemia's legation in
England

1466
First Czech printed book
published
Age of religious tolerance

1526
Beginnings of Habsburg rule
Rudolph II's Court at Prague
English refugees and visitors

1618
The Defenestration of Prague
starts the anti-Habsburg rising

1620
Volunteers sent to Bohemia

1621
English Parliament censors royal policy
The "Comenians" in England

1640
The English Revolution

1649
Execution of Charles I
Cromwell's Commonwealth
Wars against France
England's economic penetration into Central Europe

1714
The Hanoverians

1619
Frederick elected King of Bohemia

1620
Defeat of independent Bohemia

1634
Death of Wallenstein

1641—42
Comenius in England

1648
Treaty of Westphalia
Economic and cultural decline of Bohemia and Slovakia
Turkish wars and wars against France
Plans of cooperation
Manufactories in Bohemia
Trade with England and America begins

1745
Highland Rebellion
Industrial Revolution

1776
Declaration of American
Independence

1781
Czech National Revival begins
Wars against France

1789
French Revolution, Wars against
France

1805
Battle of Trafalgar

1805
Battle of Slavkov (Austerlitz)
Industrial Revolution begins

1832
First Reform Bill

1832
Bowring's Cheskian Anthology

1848
Chartists greet Czech national
movement
Reign of Queen Victoria

1848
*Revolution and Counter-revolution
in Central Europe*

1864
First International founded
in London

1864
Shakespeare Festival in Prague
Industrialization of Bohemia and
Moravia
Czech music acclaimed in England

1876
Czech working-class émigrés in
London

1906
E. Beneš publishes his articles on social conditions in England

1914
First World War begins

1914
First World War begins

1916
School of Slavonic Studies founded in London

1918
Establishment of independent Czechoslovakia

1919
Treaty of Versailles
Pro-German campaign in Britain in the twenties

1919
Attempts at an agrarian reform
Opposition of German landowners
Anglophile attitude of Czech intelligentsia
Sudeten Germans turn Nazi

1933
Decline of democratic Europe begins

1938
The Munich Crisis

1938
The Munich Crisis

1939
Second World War begins

1939
Occupation of Czechoslovakia
Beginnings of the Czechoslovak resistance movement

1940
Czechoslovaks take part in the Battle of Britain
Lidice Shall Live campaign

1940
Exiled government established

1942
Lidice destroyed

1944
Invasion

1945
End of World War II

1948
Cold War Period begins
Renewal of cultural contact in late fifties

1964
Shakespeare Anniversary

1943
Soviet-Czechoslovak Friendship Treaty

1944
National Rising in Slovakia

1945
Liberation of Czechoslovakia
Government of National Front in Czechoslovakia

1948
University celebrations in Prague

1949
First Five-Year Plan started

1960
Constitution of Socialist Republic of Czechoslovakia

1964
Shakespeare celebrations

Index